D0872515

# Can Tommy Come Out and Play?

## *My Adventures in Education*

by Thomas H. Shade

*I dedicate this book to my
wonderful wife, Delores, who has
provided the love, wisdom, and
guidance that I have needed.*

# Acknowledgements

For the most part, this book is derived from my experiences with hundreds of children, teachers, staff, parents, and friends. It is based mostly on my memory, and I apologize for any errors or omissions.

I am grateful to all those people who called or wrote to share a story. Regretfully, I could not use them all.

A belated thanks to my very good friend and co-worker, Bobby Garver, who discussed this book with me from her hospital bed just 10 days before she died. As was always the case with Bobby, she was more concerned about the well-being of my wife and me than she was about discussing her own illness. God bless you, Bobby.

Thanks to my wife, Delores, my son, John, and a very good friend, Wayne Main, for their help, expertise, and patience, in guiding me through the rigors and trauma of Personal Computing 101; thanks also for their help with proofreading and the making of hard copies.

A great big thanks to Julie Summers Walker, a student of mine when I first began teaching, who has edited this book with enthusiasm and who has provided me with much encouragement.

Deep thanks to Jose and Pat Salaverri, owners of Mealey's Restaurant, for letting our kids know that their random acts of kindness were appreciated.

Much appreciation to parent Gail Winer for the wonderful sentiments she expressed in her letter.

Thanks to Mary Spanberger for being a good friend and a great PTA president, for ironing my sport coat in the laminator the day the lapel wouldn't lay flat, and for encouraging me to continue the Parent Volunteer shows when I came to New Market Elementary School.

Many thanks to Heather Stewart for converting this Word document into the proper printing files and for designing the cover.

Lastly, to all those who have helped me in one fashion or another but have not been acknowledged—and I know there must be many— I apologize.

*A child's spirit can be
undernourished as well as his body.
Your faith and your courage and your love
are Grade A goods for your child's spirit.*

*Children need models not critics.*

*A child regards your cheery smile as
an evidence that you are on his side,
so he relaxes and is happier.*

*A teacher affects eternity;
he can never tell where his influence stops.*

*The first object of any act of learning...
is that it should serve us in the future.*

Anonymous

# Early Influences

My getting into education evolved in a strange kind of way. I was very happy with my accounting job—naive perhaps, but happy. I came home from work one night and told my wife some exciting news. I was working for a local accounting firm, and since I had not yet completed all the course work to sit for the CPA exam, I was being paid their minimum wage. My pay gradually increased, but not as fast as the level and complexity of work I was given to accomplish. One month, I happened to notice the billings that were sent to our clients. I was low on the pay scale, but my time was being billed out at CPA rates. I am sure that I realized that the firm was making considerable money from my accounts, but still, it pleased me that the company could get the highest rate for my work. Besides, my boss was continually letting me know that I had a great future in accounting.

I never told them about the constant headaches I got from all of the close work.

In the meantime, all was well at home. My wife and I had been married just a few years; we did not yet have any children; she was a music teacher in the school system, and I was on an upward career path. But my eye strain and headaches wouldn't stop. As much as I liked this job, I came home every night with throbbing headaches. They were so painful that I began questioning whether or not I wanted to do this type of work for the rest of my life.

We lived in a modest little home, our first. On one side, our neighbor was a widow, at least 80 years old, who still mowed her grass, shoveled snow, and did all the many chores that go with maintaining a home. Mrs. Cline was amazing. On the other side lived a family that included two beautiful little girls, ages 4 and 8, named Tammy and Robin. These girls and I became playmates, soul mates, and very good friends. They were the children my wife and I did not yet have. Mostly, the girls and I played school. Robin was the teacher; Tammy and I were the students. This went on for months. Every evening, those two little girls would come to our front door and ring the doorbell; my wife would usually answer, and their first comment was always the same: "Mrs.

Shade, can Tommy come out and play?" And I did. One evening, when I came back inside, my wife said to me, "Tom, have you ever considered getting a job working with kids all the time?" I replied, "Never!"

I said never, but I believe it was because I was unsure of myself, not very confident. I had not been a conscientious student in high school. In fact, I failed my junior year. There were 16 students in my junior class.

Of the 16, six males were retained. I had been attending the local Catholic school. After the retention, I transferred to Frederick High School, barely squeaking by during my last two years. I never encountered drugs and never got into trouble with the law, but I became one of many who drove their cars up, down, and around the main streets in town for hours at a time. We were never bored; at least, that's what we told each other. We came up with many creative ways to buy beer illegally. I challenged authority, both at school and at home. I respected my peers only, many of whom had no more ambition, energy, or inclination to succeed than I did. When I graduated from high school, I weighed 127 pounds. Four years later, I weighed 212 pounds, from drinking too much beer and eating at all hours of the day. Years later, when I began working with 14- and 15-year-olds at the middle school, many of whom exhibited some of the same negative characteristics and tendencies as I had, I remember thinking to myself, I *know* what they are going through; I *recognize* their frustration with authority at home and school; I *can see* myself, and I *can help* them.

I had taken some earlier accounting courses, but after observing how excited I got playing school with these little girls, my wife encouraged me to consider teaching as my main occupation.

We started cautiously. I began to take some evening education courses at the local community college. I did this for two years, received my AA degree, and then we made the plunge. I would commute to the University of Maryland every day and take the required courses I needed for a teaching degree. I quit my day job but continued to do some part-time work at night with the same accounting firm. The classwork was not difficult for me. In fact, the only thing that even stressed me a little bit was the drive back and forth every day. My wife Delores' part of the bargain was to work her full-time job (we had no other significant income), tend to our now first-born, fix meals, and take care of the house. I helped, but nowhere close to what could be considered equal. I felt guilty every time someone would tell me what a wonderful thing I was doing by giving up my work and going back to school to pursue a new career. Nothing I did came anywhere close to the sacrifices that Delores made.

In the middle of my last year at the University of Maryland, my accounting boss made me a tremendous offer to come back and work full-time with him. If I would give up this education business, he would pay all expenses for the completion of my accounting degree, including the expense to sit for the CPA exam, and give us money to live on until I was finished everything.

We took about a week to mull over and consider his wonderful offer, but, after all the *what ifs* were considered, I knew what I wanted to do.

*We can, whenever and wherever we choose,*
*successfully teach all children whose schooling*
*is of interest to us. We already know more than*
*we need in order to do this. Whether we do it*
*must finally depend on how we feel about the*
*fact that we haven't done it so far.*

Ron Edmonds
Research on Effective Schools

# Introduction

Teachers are not allowed to strike in the state of Maryland. It was the 1967-1968 school year, and my wife was a music teacher in Frederick County. Having spent the previous 10 years as an accountant, and not making any significant progress in the field, I was now completing the requisite courses and student teaching to get my degree in elementary/middle school education. Student teaching was my last required subject, and I was excited. It was early May, a warm day, and because teachers were not happy with the contract being "offered" by the system, and because they couldn't strike, most of the teachers in the county called in sick and congregated at the local armory building to begin what they called a Work Study Day. Even though I was not yet an employee of the system, I attended. There were discussions, cheers, placard-waving, speeches, and a chorus of boos when high-ranking school officials showed up. I watched and observed with astonishment. When the president of the Principals' Association, Oliver Crouse, stood in the middle of hundreds of teachers and announced that his group was 100 percent in support of the teachers, the crowd went crazy. I, too, was hooked. I wanted to be a teacher. Two months later, at the age of 31, I signed my teaching contract for an annual salary of $5,200 and was assigned to Parkway Elementary School in downtown Frederick, Maryland.

## Only A Teacher?

*I Am A Teacher!* What I do and say will be absorbed by young minds who will echo these images across the ages. My lessons will be immortal, affecting people yet unborn, people I will never see or know. The future of the world is in my classroom today, a future with the potential for good or bad. The pliable minds of tomorrow's leaders will be molded either artistically or grotesquely by what I do.

Several future presidents will be learning from me today; so will the great writers of the next decades and so will all the so-called ordinary people who will make the decisions in a democracy. I must never forget these same young people could be the thieves and murderers of the future.

*ONLY a Teacher?* Thank God I have a calling to the greatest profession of all! I must be vigilant every day lest I lost one fragile opportunity to improve tomorrow.

Ivan Welton Fitzwater

# In the Beginning

I taught fifth-grade my first year and sixth-grade my second year as an elementary school teacher. My first principal was T. Fenn Rider. I liked him a lot, but I thought he was a little strange. (This wise comment comes to you from someone who was called "that old Sphinx face" by a teacher some three years later.)

We had Truck Day at our school my first year. There were fire trucks, police cars, tanks, 18-wheelers, backhoes, tractors, a helicopter, and much more. Kids crawled in, around, and over everything. If a piece of equipment was capable of making a noise, then the kids made it happen. Someone who lived near the school called the police department in the early afternoon to complain about the racket. Headquarters radioed the patrol car nearest to the school, and the officer was told to respond to a complaint of excessive noise at Parkway Elementary School. The patrol officer had to ask the dispatcher to repeat the message, as some very excited second-graders were setting off his siren repeatedly. When asked where he was, the officer sheepishly reported that he and his patrol car were smack in the middle of Parkway Elementary's Truck Day.

In the late 1960s, I did things in my classroom that could not be done today. It was a few days before school would begin for the 1968-1969 school year. A veteran teacher asked me if I had been to the bookroom yet. I told her no, and she suggested that I get there fast if I wanted relatively new reading and math textbooks. "Wait too late," she said, "and you'll be using books written 20 years ago."

There were specific units to be taught to fifth- and sixth-graders and, other than that, we were on our own to find appropriate books and materials. Timelines, goals, objectives, and skills to be learned and mastered at each grade level, as we have today, just didn't exist then. The teacher next door to me was Barbara Norris. We were both fascinated by a book we had read to our class, *The Phantom Tollbooth*, by Norton Juster. We asked for permission to use this book as our language arts/reading book for five weeks. I felt that we could teach all the language arts skills our students needed to learn by planning our units from this book. My students were having a problem with learning and retaining language arts skills and I felt that it might be because I was teaching them in a vacuum. When I began teaching writing and mechanical skills within the context of the books that they were reading, the students seemed to grasp the skills much better.

The book was excellent for checking for comprehension. The main character in the book, a boy named Milo, drove his pretend car through a tollbooth, and once through, all kinds of exciting and adventurous things began to happen. He was told that someone had kidnapped Princess Rhyme and Princess Reason and unless he helped to find them, there would be no more rhyme nor reason in the land. He crossed the Mountains of Ignorance, the Foothills of Confusion, and the Sea of Knowledge, searched the towns of Digitopolis and Dictionopolis, and even spent two days in the Doldrums. The whole book was a high-level play on words. I didn't know if the excitement of the kids during those five weeks was normal or not. I remember our school secretary, Joyce Mason, remarking to me that not one kid had been absent from my class or Mrs. Norris' class since we started that unit.

Ten or 15 years after we had planned our language arts unit around *The Phantom Tollbooth*, the book was the subject of some controversy. According to the People For The American Way Foundation, *The Phantom Tollbooth* was locked in a reference collection at the Boulder, Colorado, Public Library. That meant that the book was not accessible by regular means. By request, a library official would unlock the reference room door and allow children to check out the book. This was in 1989, and resulted after school officials received two objections to the book. There were two other books locked up in the reference room at the same time. Librarians considered *The Giving Tree*, by Shel Silverstein, sexist; deemed *The Phantom Tollbooth*, by Norton Juster, poor fantasy; and *Charlie and the Chocolate Factory*, by Roald Dahl, was alleged to espouse a poor philosophy of life. These books were subsequently released from the locked-up reference rooms and children were once again allowed to enjoy these classic stories.

### Less Talk, More Action

It was April 1970, and I was in my second year of teaching. The class was social studies. We had just finished reading an article dealing with poverty areas. This led us to discuss other subjects. The kids were into this discussion, and one suggested that they become an *action* group rather than a *talk* group. Our topics included poverty, crime, housing, conservation, pollution, the war in Vietnam, drugs, and health hazards. We established goals for each of the topics and discussed whether we had the means to accomplish our goals. We had no unit plan and very few materials to guide us.

The students brought in everything. They planned bulletin boards, wrote letters, and decided among themselves how their group would function. In the 1970s, all we knew was that we had to work together. Today, we call that Cooperative Learning, which is a method of learning that takes advantage of the numerous benefits that result from student-to-student interactions. Cooperative Learning consists of many components. It fosters interdependence, teaching the skill of relying on one another collectively for a positive outcome. Each child has something specific for which he or she is accountable. We came up with a very ambitious list of activities to accomplish. They were:

- Tour a poverty area
- Collect canned food for the poor
- Have a speaker address the group about drugs
- Tour the local state police barracks
- Plant a windbreak on school property
- Correspond with local businessmen relative to their activities to combat pollution
- Arrange for a speech by then-Maryland State Senator Goodloe Byron.
- Visit City Hall and meet the mayor
- Conduct live smoking tests using a machine developed for that purpose
- Clean school grounds and the local creek — Carroll Creek — of litter.
- Set up a discussion of the Vietnam War
- Conduct an action campaign in the school on topics such as pollution, drugs, juvenile crimes, smoking, etc.

Almost everything on this list was accomplished. The idea for the clean-up campaign, incidentally, predated the announcement of national Earth Day activities by some two months. While going through my boxes of materials from the past 30 years, I found notes written to me by some of the students. Their reactions were: ".... school is really fun;." "It's fun to learn this way;" "Doing it ourselves is much more fun;" "I didn't understand much about these problems before, but I do now."

Even though their reactions stressed *fun*, the unit was important as a hands-on learning experience. Kids are not a whole lot different now than they were 30 years ago, except that they, and their parents, have a lot more things with which to occupy themselves. Teachers worked very hard then and they work very hard now, but I think today's teachers get more frustrated because of all the demands placed on them.

I could not teach the *Tollbooth* unit and the Social Issues unit today because there is no room in the schedule to add extra topics. There have been too many local- and state-mandated units added to our teaching schedule in the last 30 years. Much gets added but nothing gets deleted. One of the lessons I learned as a new teacher when we did all those action activities in our Social Issues unit was that 10-, 11-, and 12-year-olds have an interest in and understanding of events in their world when things are presented to them in a meaningful way. We couldn't just read about the Vietnam War, juvenile crime, and drugs in the '60s and '70s. We visited the state police barracks and heard directly about apprehension techniques of juvenile offenders; we invited Maryland State Senator Goodloe Byron to our class and asked questions about politics and Vietnam; and we brought a smoking machine into our room, observed as it "smoked" dozens of brands of cigarettes, stared with amazement at the tar and nicotine stains deposited on the filters corresponding to each cigarette, and equated the filters to our lungs.

I was also interested in the students having a pride in, and getting a grasp of, our own local area, and how people and buildings in our town and county had historical relevance to what has happened, what is happening now, and what could happen. We took several walking tours of downtown Frederick. Parkway Elementary School was very conveniently located. Once, when we were discussing presidents, the topic suddenly became more relevant right after we took one bus trip and one walking tour. We had been discussing presidents who had visited and stayed in Frederick. When we went to Rose Hill Manor, where Maryland's first governor, Thomas Johnson, had lived, and also where he died, we learned that George Washington had visited him there in that building when Johnson was sick. The students were also impressed to learn that Abraham Lincoln had visited Frederick several times.

We walked to two of those places, a house on Record Street and the old Baltimore & Ohio Railway station on All Saints Street. I told the students that, to the best of my knowledge, those were the only two presidents who had come to Frederick, although in 1971, Richard Nixon had been in Frederick to visit the biological warfare center at Fort Detrick and announced at that time that Detrick would be converted to the Frederick Cancer Research Center.

Toward the end of the second year, I was finishing the final draft of my masters' thesis and had it stored in my file cabinet. One evening, I received a telephone call telling me that Parkway School was on fire. I rushed to the school and was shocked to see flames and smoke at every window. I panicked and did a very dumb thing. I ran into the school and to my second floor classroom, trying without success to push the smoke away. I retrieved my thesis and started back down the stairs. The smoke was so thick as I was trying desperately to retrace my steps, that I started to wonder if I was going to make it down. With tears in my eyes and coughing and choking from the heavy smoke, I crawled the last 30 yards or so on my hands and knees and eventually made it to the front door and fresh air. After asking me if I was all right, a firefighter reprimanded me for what seemed like forever. To add to my embarrassment, standing next to him was Mrs. Mary Condon Hodgson, Board of Education president. Although she expressed appropriate concern, somehow I had the impression that she didn't think that I was too swift.

*If you feel secure,*
*do what you already know*
*how to do.*

*But if you want to grow, go to*
*the cutting edge of your*
*competence which means a*
*temporary loss of security.*

*So...whenever you don't quite*
*know what you are*
*doing, know that you are growing!*

Anonymous

# On My Way

By the end of my second year of teaching, I began to think of school administration as the next step.

Our county used to have Saturday morning workshops to help prepare wannabe administrators. Usually, we would be asked to respond to questions by telling how we would resolve the presented problem. The director of elementary schools 30 years ago was Charlotte Smith. She was my role model. She was the most patient, kind, giving, and encouraging person I had ever met. She was a master at giving constructive criticism. She would say, "Tom, you are not going to get through any interviews if you begin the answer to every question by saying, 'I don't know if this is right, but'..."

I had my first official interview for the position of vice-principal (they are now referred to as assistant principals) in June 1970. On hindsight, I shouldn't have gotten the job. I wasn't yet a master teacher; I didn't know the curriculum well enough, and most importantly, I wasn't ready. But I was 32 years old; I was male, and back then more than 80 percent of school administrators were male. Bob Humphrey, principal at New Market Elementary School, hired me. I learned more from him on the job than I could have learned from a textbook. He allowed me to make decisions, but he would talk to me later about the wisdom of some of them. I loved administration but it took me several years to admit it publicly. I remember telling my students and their parents that I would much rather be in the classroom teaching. But the reality was that I wanted to lead a school, and I wanted — and needed — the 12-month salary that came with it.

Observing and supervising teachers and responding to parents' concerns were not always as clear-cut as the questions in my Saturday morning administrator workshops. At the end of my very first day as an elementary vice-principal, the telephone rang. I said "Hello," and the very loud and very angry voice on the other end said, "Who in the hell at that school is in charge of f--- ups?" I gulped, held out the telephone, and said, "Mr. Humphrey, phone call for you."

14

I had another experience with the F word two days later. A child had been sent to my office for writing "f--- you" in the dust on the windowsill. He admitted it, and I did the appropriate reprimand, which included having his parents sign a note indicating that they were aware of what had happened and what I had done. The boy's mother showed up at school the next day and immediately told me that she would sign no such note, and also said, "For your information, my son did not even know that word until *you* came to this school."

Mr. Humphrey told me that one of my tasks was to observe teachers, write an observation report, and go over it with the teacher.

Betty Sponseller was a tough lady, with 30 years' teaching experience, and I started in her room with my observations. Betty didn't have a whole lot of patience or concern for brand-new, mistake-prone teachers or administrators. Her deep, gruff voice bellowed out like a master sergeant's. (In fact, during the Korean War, she *was* a master sergeant.) I was not in Betty's room with my clipboard more than five minutes when Betty proclaimed, in her loud, husky voice, which I was certain could be heard by every teacher along the hallway, "Mr. Shade, I will not have a young squirt observing me while I am teaching."

I got up and walked out. That afternoon, after the students had left for the day, I went back. I said, "Betty, Mr. Humphrey hired me to do a job, and I plan to be back tomorrow morning to observe you and if you want to go around and around with me, we can do that. Also, I expect you to tell your students that you were just kidding, or whatever else you choose to tell them, but let them know that you respect the job that I have to do and that I will be back today to do it." Early the next morning, I was called to Mr. Humphrey's office and Betty was already there. She told Bob in front of me that I had come into her room and sat there like a "Sphinx-face." (I have to admit that that was probably true, partly because I was intimidated by her and partly because I have been told by others that they never know what I am thinking because my expression doesn't change. I tried to practice smiling more, but it always seemed to me to be contrived on my part.)

To my delight, Mr. Humphrey supported my position. To my great surprise, Betty would later ask to come to teach for me at Green Valley.

"A lot of superintendents ask me what I'd look for if I were picking elementary school teachers.... If I had to narrow it down to one characteristic, I would always hire teachers whom I would want to have dinner with. I would look for people who are capable of making the world seem joyful, people who are a delight to be with, people who are contagiously amusing human beings. To me, that's more important than almost anything else. I would put the emphasis on the capability to create contagious enthusiasm for life. There are a lot of teachers like that, but not enough."

Jonathan Kozol
On Being A Teacher

# Principal Shade at Green Valley
## 1971 - 1978

During the spring of 1971, I wrote the appropriate letter indicating my interest in applying for a principal's position. I thought that if a small-school position became available, it would be a perfect opportunity. If not, I would wait until the next year. To my surprise, I was called in for an interview. The first question I was asked was, "Why do you want to be a principal?" I had made up my mind earlier that there would be no conditional answers nor would there be any hesitation on my part. I immediately and forthrightly told the panel that the principalship is a mountain I wanted to climb, and there were many things (which I enumerated) that I wanted to do, but couldn't in the number-two slot. I had to be the number-one man. As I walked out of the interview, I exchanged smiles with Charlotte Smith. I interpreted her nod not to mean I would get the job but that she was proud of the approach I took to answering the questions.

I found out later that there was only one vacant position available, and that would be the brand-new open-space Green Valley Elementary School. I also knew that a very capable and experienced administrator wanted Green Valley. In the second week of August, I got the call informing me that Green Valley was my school. The new school would open the day after Labor Day, in three weeks.

A neighboring county was interviewing the veteran principal who had wanted Green Valley. Green Valley was his preference, and school officials wanted him. He had given them an ultimatum that if he was not appointed by July 15, he would withdraw his name from consideration. On July 16, he accepted a position in Montgomery County. Our school system thought that by waiting until August 15 to announce the principal, they could save a few thousand dollars in salary. They saved more than they anticipated, because they got me cheap. But they lost a very good administrator. Even though I benefited, I never understood their logic.

I told Charlotte Smith that this move would be educational suicide for me. She said she would help me, and she did.

There are a zillion things that have to be done to open a new school. I also had to hire the staff for this 700-student school.

No veteran teachers in their right minds were requesting transfers to this school, because, one, they didn't know in advance who their boss would be, and two, teachers were leery of open-space school buildings. I survived all of this, because, as I told Charlotte later, I didn't know what I was doing, and I didn't have the slightest idea what I was supposed to be worried about since I had never been in this position. A few teachers who wanted to be closer to their homes did transfer, and the rest I hired by September 1.

We opened with more than 50 teachers, and the average age of our staff was 26. That included one teacher who was over 50. Our school was open space, and I was determined that the staff would be trained accordingly, and we would live and practice the open philosophy. All of the research I had read about open space indicated that asking teachers to meet, agree, think, argue, and then work together as a total collaborative team was a very difficult and sensitive process. Teachers couldn't just think and plan for themselves in an open setting. Sometimes, the voice level got high during team meetings, but consensus was the goal and was usually achieved before the team door opened.

## Without Walls

Making decisions as a team, working side by side without walls, being able to see hundreds of kids at a glance, as well as all the teachers, kids lying on the floor, reading, writing, discussing—this was open-space philosophy at work. Phil Brohawn was putting the finishing touches on his Poetry Corner, located right in the middle of his open area; Susan Sherald was busy hanging streamers from the ceiling; Stuart Stein was writing student names in his creative writing journals; Florence Awkard was just standing back, watching intently, and taking it all in. Florence had taught at New Market for 34 years and had asked me about transferring to Green Valley. She had said she was curious about open space. Could she come with me for one year? Then she would retire. I made lots of mistakes over the years, but this was not going to be one of them. I needed Florence's wisdom, experience, coolness, and sense of humor. Plus, she was one fantastic teacher. She could help me with all those brand-new, wet-behind-the-ears young teachers, such as Phil Brohawn, Kathy Hartsock, Donna Hauver, Fred Barnette, Michele Krantz, and many more.

I became a cheerleader. I coaxed, praised, and pressured — whatever it took to get us to come together as a total staff team.

I sat in on a meeting of Florence's team one day and began to offer some unsolicited opinions. Florence turned to me and said, "Tom, why don't you go to your office, put your feet up on your desk, and practice principaling. We will stay here and do what we have to do." As the young teachers on her team stared at her with amazement, I walked out of their area and went to my office. Florence, God bless her soul, stayed with me at Green Valley for six years before she retired.

We weren't ready, but we opened on time. I remained at Green Valley from 1971 to 1978. There were many memorable experiences-some I cherish; others I'd rather forget.

- A few weeks after we opened, a parent came to the school and asked if she could look around, which she did. Then she came back to the office, eyes filled with tears, picked up a phone, called her husband and, in front of everyone, said, "Richard, you have to come up here and see this goddamn barn."
- Another lady came to see me, upset with a decision I had made, and started our conversation by saying, "I've checked it out with a Board of Education member—12 people applied to be the principal of this school and you were ranked number 12. He doesn't understand how you got this job, and neither do I."
- I saved a lot of notes that I received over the years. This is one: "Mr. Shade, our noses are numb. Could we have some more heat, please?" signed The Boys and Girls in Miss Mack's First Grade Class. "p.s. We love you, Mr. Shade. You are handsome."
- In the 1970s, teachers received sick and business leave only, and there were very specific reasons for using the business leave, of which recreational and social use was not one of them. I had told teachers that since they were not required to state a reason on their leave request form, to leave that line blank; don't write it and don't tell me why any time you request business leave. I had approved a business leave request one day, and the next day, the teacher came into my office to tell me why she was taking leave. I asked her not to tell me. She said, "Tom, you're a nice guy, and I want you to know that my development is having a block party tomorrow and I am in

charge of refreshments." I said, "Judy, I wish you hadn't told me that, because now I can't approve the leave request." We went back and forth, and I wouldn't budge. In my mind, she had crossed over the line. As she walked out of my office, she turned, glared, and then said, "Tom, I just want you to know; you're a prick of a principal." She shut the door and the chair my vice principal was sitting on fell to the floor. Delmar Rippeon was rolling on the floor, laughing the whole time.

- The worst possible thing happened at Green Valley. I was a pall-bearer at the funerals of two of my students. One had an incurable illness; the other, without looking, rode his bike down his driveway, into the street.

- We were about six months into our first year. I had just finished observing my second-grade teachers. They were wonderful, hard-working teachers. At our monthly administrators' meetings, we were being advised not to mark our teachers too high; they might rest on their laurels and not work as hard. So, for each one of them, I marked *satisfactory* in several areas. They felt that they deserved higher marks. So, for one solid week, they all wore handmade badges on their shirts and dresses, which stated, "Happiness Is Being Marked *Satisfactory* By Mr. Shade!"

- To celebrate warm weather and springtime, we began an annual outdoor program. Grades and teams would parade, holding up banners made by kids. We culminated with each class displaying their craft and artwork. Because I wasn't creative enough to think of a clever name, we simply called it our May Day Program. It was art, music, and physical education's day to celebrate their programs. Students wrote invitations to dignitaries. Student Michelle Bassett wrote one of the invitations to Dr. John Carnochan, superintendent of schools. (Twenty years later, Michelle would be the mother of several students attending New Market Elementary, and I would be their principal.) Michelle's invitation read:

MAY DAY PROGRAM

It would really be grand
If you came to Green Valley's
"May Day Program."
It's a time that is flirty,
May first at one-thirty.

It can only be seen
On the hill on the green.
And if it rains
We can't open the gate

So May eighth will be
The rainy day date.


A few days later came this reply:

Although I know you don't want it to rain
On the first day of May,
It won't be convenient for me to be
With you that day.
If you have to postpone because
The grass is wet,
I'll come on the eighth,
And enjoy it, I bet.

John Carnochan, Superintendent
April 25, 1972


On the third year of this event, and just before it was to begin, I received a telephone call from "downtown" stating that a parent had called expressing great concern that Green Valley was celebrating a communist holiday. I had heard of May Day celebrations in communist China, but I didn't see them as being in philosophical conflict with ours. I apologized and changed our name to the Green Valley Spring Festival. I kind of adopted this attitude throughout my career. I was always very careful about picking my battles. I was never the "I'm in charge, we'll do it my way" type. It was too easy to apologize and move on to more important things.

By the fourth year, Green Valley was really growing. Opening with 650 students in a 700-capacity building, we now had 965 students and 12 portable classrooms. But even with the growth, we were being asked almost weekly to allow visitors from our county and outside our county to come and talk to us about scheduling and operating a totally open school. I'd like to share parts of a letter I received from Colleen Garrett, a Frederick County administrator, on March 24, 1975.

"Dear Tom,

Thank you for letting us visit your school on Friday. I was so impressed with the smooth operation of Green Valley. The students were all involved in some activity—either small group or independent work. It was obvious the students there knew what was expected of them. Your school truly reflects the 'Open Space' philosophy. I think that the key to your success lies in first of all, your enthusiasm and belief in what you are doing, your guidance, and the BIG FACTOR...the way you have your teachers working as teams with the 'Agenda' idea. I think your faculty probably has a very close relationship, because unless each member of the team pulls his load, open space just won't work. Tom, you really made our inservice day a worthwhile experience. I especially loved your idea of the 'Happy Gram.' I hope you share that idea with your fellow principals. Then, Frederick County would have the happiest parents around!!! Green Valley represents so much time and effort on your part...that I wish all those opposed to Open Space could visit your school before they make the decision to 'put the walls back' or go open space. Thanks again for a great day."

It was right after this that T. Meade Felton, director of community relations for the school system, came to visit. Many parents in all open space schools were expressing concerns and misgivings about the concept. Our system had sent out a survey letter on open space to teachers and parents, and Meade had come to share the results. He told me that 77 percent of the people returning the surveys from other areas of the county expressed total dissatisfaction with open space, but the parents and teachers at Green Valley were satisfied to the tune of 86 percent. Although *we* were happy with the results, our board of education began almost immediately, as funds became available, to put walls up in the schools. Meade also told me that the people downtown were amazed that the Green Valley parents would support this controversial issue. Many Green Valley parents had come from Montgomery County. The Board of Education considered those parents difficult because they seemed to be demanding Montgomery

County services at Frederick County tax rates. He added that he doubted that I would ever be promoted above principal level because the "people downtown" felt that my communication skills with parents — especially these very demanding and vocal Green Valley parents — were better served at the school level. I didn't buy that then, and I don't buy it now. I treated parents the same in all the schools I was in. But his prediction did turn out to be true.

### Open, But Overcrowded

An overcrowded, open-space school is a legitimate concern. Seeing and hearing good news about your children is a delight for all parents. I bought a camera. I set a goal of five to eight students per day. I would walk around and "catch kids working." I would send the picture home with a brief note telling the parents how proud I was of their child. I concluded each note by inviting the parents to come in, look around, and talk about their child's program. I encouraged teachers to send "Happy Grams" home, at least one a week for each child. As soon as a parent walked in the front door, I would approach him or her and say something positive about his or her child. It could have been anything; maybe I sat with them at lunch that day or heard them give an interesting report in their classroom, or thanked them for helping smaller children get off the bus. The important thing for me was to let parents know that I knew who their child was and I liked him or her.

I could address more than 95 percent of our kids by their first name. I didn't set out to do that. It came naturally because I simply liked to talk to kids, and just like all of us, they liked to hear people call them by their first name. When a child went home after school and said, "Mommy, Daddy, Mr. Shade sat with me at lunch today," or "Mr. Shade knows who I am; he spoke to me in the hallway and said my name," that's a positive experience. I know I would have felt good if my children's principals treated my children that way. Administrators are very busy people, but somehow they need to look down and see who is walking beside them and let that child know that they think he or she is very important. I rarely ate in the staff lounge. Many kids, especially the younger ones, would be wary of some adult approaching them at lunchtime, asking them if I could sit with them. But I loved the challenge.

I love grapes, so I would check to see who had grapes, and if so, I would tell them that the grapes might be poisonous and that I should check one to make sure. Even the youngest child knew that his or her parent would not give them poisonous grapes to eat. They would look at me funny or maybe even laugh, but they would almost always let me check their grapes. Once they did, we became best friends. Or I would approach a group of kids, ask them if I could sit with them to eat. I would tell them I couldn't find my Scooby Doo lunchbox and I needed company today. (I still have now grown-up kids stop me at the local mall and ask if I am still checking grapes or if I have found my Scooby Doo lunchbox.) Maybe six to 12 kids would have notes in their lunchboxes. I would walk up and ask if I could read their note from home. Very dramatically, I would read each note. Always it would be telling the kid to eat all his lunch, work hard in school, I love you very much, see you later, love, Mom. And then I would proclaim with amazement, "Would you look right here; your mommy wrote something in invisible ink." "*What does it say, Mr. Shade?*" It says, "P.S. Say hello to that handsome Mr. Shade." And the kids would roar. "*Why can't we see it, Mr. Shade?*" "Because only mommies and principals can write and read invisible ink." More best friends.

This eventually got the best of me. By the end of the week, instead of four or five kids having notes, 25 kids would have them and they would be waving them in the air. "Mr. Shade, Mr. Shade, did my mommy write anything in invisible ink today?" By this time, the person on lunch duty would be announcing over the intercom, "Would Mr. Shade's table quiet down a little bit?" One day, I sat next to a first-grade boy, noticed he had a note, and I asked him if I could read it "Yes, Mr. Shade," he said "but don't read that invisible part; my mommy doesn't even know you." And I didn't. Was this silly? Sure it was. Was I acting like a kid myself? Sure I was. Did I have fun doing it? I sure did. But for all you wannabe administrators out there, I can't count how many times that parents have come into the office, angry about something, and if they ended up seeing me, they would invariably start the conversation with Mom saying, "I had to buy grapes for Sarah's lunch today because she wants you to check them." Or, "I had to write a note to put in Sarah's lunchbox today because she wants you to read it." I would guess that 80 percent or more of my conferences were defused before we even started talking.

## Parent Volunteers
More parents began to volunteer. We probably had the largest parent volunteer base in the county. Kids were coming home happy and talk-

ing about school, and parents loved it. That's the basis for a pretty good partnership. It was also the beginning of a program that is still going strong long after my retirement, some 25 years after its inception.

Call it bribery, call it begging, call it whatever you want, but I wanted to do something extra special for our parent volunteers that would help to ensure that they would be back next year and also recruit others to help them. With a lot of help from Peg Russell and Pete Storm, we began a Parent Volunteer Night that started with our staff preparing and serving a spaghetti dinner, followed by entertainment by the staff.

I had the habit of running ideas past teachers whose thoughts I not only respected but whose support I needed if the idea was to succeed. As I had expected, some were in full approval; others would go along but were nervous about the idea of getting up on the stage to perform. I was not sure myself if it was fair to ask the staff to work extra hours after school and at night in order to accomplish this. I finally decided that I would present the idea to everybody and be prepared to accept whatever answer they gave me. I don't think I was that surprised when they overwhelmingly accepted the idea.

Open-space schools were controversial, and I knew I needed parent support. I encouraged parents to volunteer every chance they got. I asked them to come to volunteer orientation meetings, meet the teachers and instructional aides, observe what was going on in the school with the students, ask questions, hear the answers from us (not from a neighbor), get to know their child's classmates, meet other parents, study the schedule for everyday activities as well as for testing times, ask about our homework policy, post the menu when it came home every Friday, and check the messages to parents from the principal at the bottom of the menu. They showed up in huge numbers.

As a reward for volunteering so many hours, I wanted parents and grandparents to receive a special thank-you at the end of the year, more than the traditional cookie and a glass of punch. We decorated our cafeteria with thank-you banners, provided decorated tables for four-, six-, and eight-person seating, and presented special handmade gifts to our volunteers when they came in that evening. They were escorted to their candle-lit table, and served a pre-dinner drink of iced tea, coffee, or soda. All the staff showed up and either worked in the kitchen preparing the dishes or in the main room serving our guests a hot spaghetti dinner. We circulated around the room, talking and laughing with all of our volunteers. After dinner, we entertained the parents with a variety of crazy acts, sang to them, and let them know that this Parent Volunteer Appreciation Night was our special way of thanking some very special people. We loved doing it; parents loved the fuss we made over them. It was a win-win situation.

I was the proud co-host and master of ceremonies of this great night for 26 consecutive years. The hall was always packed with our special guests. But I think the one thing I was most proud of was that we always had 100-percent participation and attendance from our staff.

## Good Teachers

I have been called many names over the years. I have already mentioned a few. I have been referred to as a motivator, a people person, child-centered, and child advocate. (One fellow administrator called me a super bull-shitter.) I plead guilty to all of them. I would have loved to have become a master of the curriculum, a theorist, a teacher of teachers. But I never did. So I compensated. I have many weaknesses in education, partly because I moved up too fast. I didn't have time to learn, so I surrounded myself with good people and learned to delegate.

I could always sense and know when good teaching was happening in the classroom, but I wasn't always sure why it was happening. It was the same with bad teaching. Not always, but after some particularly vexing observations, and without naming the teacher, I would go to my reading specialist, or many times, to my assistant principal and say, this is what I observed—what do you think? More than once, they would say, "You've been in so and so's room, haven't you?"

I love music, always have. I am married to a music teacher. At school, I worked with two very talented musicians, Peg Russell and Pete Storm. In 1976, they were the skilled people who helped us make a reel-to-reel slide tape of our open-space school. We had music in the background, student, teacher, and parent discussions, and some original songs written by Peg and Pete. We were invited to take our tape to surrounding counties, even some neighboring states. Our school community was proud of our school, and we wanted others to hear from our school teams. We were invited to our own Board of Education meeting. I still watch that slide show occasionally.

Before being invited to the "Board," one of its members had told a reporter in an interview how opposed she was to open-space education. I wrote her a note telling her I was offended that a board member would make a public comment like that when she had never once come to observe us, the newest open-space school. I told her that I respected her opinion but wondered why she had not responded to my invitation to visit. She never answered my note.

## Boundary Lines

Toward the end of the '70s, Green Valley had 1,000 students and 12 portable classrooms. But help was on the way. Urbana Elementary was being renovated as well as getting an addition. This was important to us because, when construction was completed, they would relieve the over-crowding at Green Valley.

While relief sounds nice, it also puts into play several other areas of unpleasantness, including changing school boundary lines and the excessing of a proportionate number of teachers relative to the number of students you are transferring to the relief school.

Changing school boundary lines presented problems in public relations. As much as parents wanted relief at their crowded school, most of them wanted some other area, some other development, some other road to be within the new school's boundary. If a new school could take 300 additional students, then the superintendent appoints a committee of staff and parents to sit down with maps and attempt to make several determinations about where these 300 kids could come from. After the committee decides on three or four possible scenarios, one or more public meetings are held to get input from the parents.

Sometimes, the recommendations are pretty obvious and the committee receives little negative feedback. Such was the case at Green Valley. Everyone knew that all the homes west and south of the school on Routes 75 and 80 were obvious choices to go to Urbana, and the homes north of Wilcom's Inn and east of the school would remain at Green Valley. It makes it pretty easy when all 300 kids you are looking for reside in a pretty compact geographical area. When New Market Elementary had to redistrict for the opening of Twin Ridge Elementary and again for the opening of Deer Crossing Elementary, it wasn't nearly as easy. The boundary lines for both schools were not as obvious. That's when the committee's recommendation meetings for parent input became tense and emotional. "Let somebody else's child move," became the rally cry for many. Usually, the emotion of the parents is fueled by what they feel is the best situation for them and their children at that time. At the night meeting to discuss which areas and developments would be transferred from New Market to Twin Ridge, many of the parents were fiercely determined to persuade the committee not to move their area to Twin Ridge. Some five years later, some of those same parents were just as adamant about not having their children transferred back to New Market when another redistricting of the same area resulted from the opening of Deer Crossing.

The principal of the sending school has mixed emotions at these meetings. While he certainly welcomes the relief his school will get, he is inwardly feeling good about the fact that so many people want to remain at his school. The principal of the receiving school, quite often a stranger to that school area, has to sit and listen to people give all the reasons for not wanting to move.

After having its night meetings, the committee goes back to work and attempts to come up with a recommendation to be made to the superintendent who makes the final decision about what to recommend to the Board of Education. I can only applaud the people who give their time to work on these sometimes thankless committees. I have been on several, and no matter how fair you try to be or how hard you try to take everybody's suggestions into consideration, the bottom line is that you are charged with making a recommendation to the superintendent and that means that some people will not be happy with it.

### Excessing

Students and parents generally do not have any idea what tension and strain there is for teachers who are in an excessing situation and for the principals who have to make the decision. Using the Twin Ridge and Deer Crossing schools as examples, New Market would lose about 500 kids to each school. These two schools opened within five years of each other. New Market Elementary was affected both times because of the tremendous number of homes built in the area in the early 1990s. The development right next door to the school, called "Smurf Village" by the kids because the houses were so small, was originally thought to be of interest only to young couples without children and retirement-age people whose children were gone. Not true by a long shot! We registered hundreds of kids from this development. The county's formula for determining staffing was one teacher per 23 students. The one-to-23 ratio was not a true reflection of class size. Back then, the ratio included specials teachers and the reading specialist. After allowing for these positions, the actual class size might be closer to 30. Today, when principals receive one to 23, the one refers to classroom teachers only. Other types of teachers are added separately. If we would indeed lose 500 kids, then simple division equates to roughly 22 teachers having to be excessed. In addition to those teachers, we would lose a proportionate number of art, music, physical education, special education, kindergarten, aides, and secretaries. The 22 are classroom teachers only.

There are some rules that apply to excessing. The rule that mattered most to most principals was the last one that stated that principals could make decisions that would be "in the best interests of the school." Some teachers didn't like that rule, but it was a very important one for principals.

Not all teachers had to be excessed. In my case, I would meet with the whole faculty, explain the situation and the numbers, tell them that it would make it a lot easier for me if many would consider placing their name voluntarily on the excess list. I would get many names that way, but not all. Some principals would use the straight LIFO method — last in-first out. That is the easy stress-free method for the principal. Also, no one could argue or charge unfairness with that method.

A few teachers' names ended up on the excess list at every school they worked. One year, I received a teacher who had been excessed from a school, and at the end of the school year with me, landed on the excess list again. This teacher came to see me and told me that her previous principal had told her that she would never have to worry about being excessed again. The principal had also told her that, unlike other principals, she only excessed her best teachers because it wasn't fair to her fellow principals to excess teachers who weren't the best. I told the teacher that was b.s. and she knew it.

Some principals came up with all kinds of attractive charts that had all kinds of information listed behind each teacher's name, the bottom line being that if you didn't get enough points, you made the excess list. In fact, I received a teacher who had been excessed by that method. I guess that method has some value because, when that same teacher appeared on my excess list the following year, she asked me why I didn't make one of those wonderful charts so that this process could be done fair and square. I told her that a chart would not have changed her situation. I don't think it's fair for principals to imply to teachers that everyone has an equal chance of staying because they are going to make a chart. I can make a chart say anything that I want it to say.

Every year, before we got relief, I always enrolled 30 to 50 new kids, which translates to two more teachers. Over a five-to-seven-year period, we're talking 10 to 14 additional teachers. And every year, my boss downtown would tell me that I would have to take my teachers from other schools' excess lists. The only time I would ever get to interview for a teacher was when they would give me additional help on the first day of school because of over-projection enrollment at the last minute, but I could pick only if the excess list had been depleted. The only time in all those years that I was allowed to get a teacher from the Teacher Transfer Request list was when I was told by Barbara Onofrey, master teacher deluxe, that she and her husband were building a home in Gettysburg, and she would be requesting a transfer. I called my boss, Sherry Collette, and pleaded with her not to make me take a replacement from the excess list. As it turned out, Steve Martin, principal of Thurmont Elementary, had a teacher who wanted to transfer closer to home. Sherry gave permission to Steve and me to affect a switch of teachers. I told Steve to level with me because he would be getting one of the best teachers I had ever hired. Steve assured me that he felt the same way about his teacher, Patty Waldron. Only time would tell if we were telling each other the truth. We were, and both schools replaced strong with strong. Patty came to New Market and did an outstanding job. She also met a young man named Steve Lockard, whom she eventually married. That was good news and bad news. Patty stayed at New Market for only a few years because my soon-to-be-next-assistant principal would be Steve, and it was felt that it would be best for both Patty and Steve if they were not in the same school.

I would encourage as many teachers as possible to volunteer to be excessed. I would tell teachers that if I got 22 volunteers, fine, the process was over. If I didn't, then I would do what I thought was best for my school. To be honest, not many teachers wanted to leave New Market for either Twin Ridge or Deer Crossing. There was a complication with the rules back then. First-year teachers could not be excessed. Veteran teachers did not think this was fair. One first-year teacher came to me in tears one day with a note in her hand. The note, with no signature, accused the first-year teacher of taking a veteran teacher's slot and told her that she should be ashamed and not let that happen. There were some veteran teachers I would have preferred, but I knew why the rule was there, and I was determined that we would follow the rule. The note was destroyed, and we went about our business.

One more thought about that whole area of summer hiring: I stated already that there was a procedure for filling vacancies over the summer. The excess list people were placed first, followed by people coming back from leave, such as maternity, leaves of absence, etc. (One thing I used to do, and so did other principals, was work *around* the rules.) Sometimes, I would go four or five years without the opportunity to interview and hire the person I wanted. The vast majority of my vacancies were due to increased enrollment projections and therefore my boss always knew how we stood with teacher needs; hence, I would always get teachers that another principal had excessed. But every once in awhile, I would get lucky. A teacher would call me, let's say, toward the end of June, and tell me that her husband has been transferred to another state, and she would not be returning in September to teach. I would ask the teacher to wait until I called her before she submitted her resignation. And then about every three or four days, I would call Human Services for whatever reason, and I would say, "Oh, by the way, how many people are still on the excess list that haven't been placed yet? Is that right? How about the 'coming back from leave' list?" I did this until I got zero for the answers to both questions. When I got zero, I would call the teacher and tell her it was time to submit the resignation. Then I would call my boss, Sherry, tell her I had a resignation coming in, and she would tell me that it was my lucky day because the last person on the leave list was placed this morning. It's not that people on leave lists are not good; it's just that I wanted the chance to interview and select my own person.

### Middle School

I had been at Green Valley for seven years, became eager for a new challenge, and decided to apply for the position of principal at the brand-new middle school under construction at New Market. I was very excited when I was told that I would be the first middle-school principal in Frederick County.

Although I was looking forward to going to a new school, I had mixed emotions about leaving Green Valley. One of my fondest memories of Green Valley was the Labor Day holiday. Because our school was so wide open, teachers at each grade level spent a great deal of time and energy transforming their assigned spaces into easily identifiable areas. The purpose was to create an exciting environment for kids to come into each day. Fifth-grade became Treasure Island; a walk into the third-grade area took you to The Enchanted Forest. Each grade-level had its own theme. It became a tradition in my family for the four of us to go to the school every year on Labor Day, the last day before school officially started, to walk around and look at each grade's creation. Dozens of dedicated teachers would also be there, providing those last-minute enhancements to their areas.

## I dreamed I stood in a studio

I dreamed I stood in a studio
and watched two sculptors there.
The clay they used was a young child's mind
and they fashioned it with care.

One was a teacher, the tools used
were books and music and art.
One was a parent with a guiding hand
and a gentle loving heart.

Day after day the teacher toiled
with a touch that was soft and sure,
While the parent labored by the teacher's side
and polished and smoothed it all.

And when at last their task was done
they were proud of what they had wrought.
For the things they had molded into the child
could neither be sold nor bought.

And each agreed they would have failed
if they had worked alone.
For behind the parent stood the school
and behind the teacher, the home.

Author Unknown

# Linganore West - New Market Middle
## 1978 - 1981

New Market Middle School was under construction and wouldn't be ready for another year.

Linganore High was bursting at the seams and needed immediate relief. At that time, Green Valley was K-6 and Linganore was 7-12. When New Market Middle was finished, it would be the first true middle school in the county, housing grades 6-8. Elementary schools would then become K-5 and high schools 9-12.

I was appointed principal of New Market Middle one year before it would open. The plan was to place Linganore's seventh grade in a separate building for one year. This would relieve Linganore Junior/Senior High School, and their seventh-grade class would enter New Market Middle the following year as its first eighth-grade class. Students in grades five and six from New Market, Liberty, and Green Valley would go to the middle school the next year.

It was decided that we would use the old Walkersville Elementary School building to house Linganore's seventh grade for one year.

It was an empty, unused building, but still in good shape.

In the spring of 1978, a meeting was held with school officials, seventh-grade parents, and myself. Transportation, the school's name, and academics were the three items on the agenda. The students would be traveling from the Linganore area to Walkersville. It was agreed that the kids would be picked up from their homes and proceed to Walkersville by taking Route 75 north to Liberty, and then 26 west to 194. Just outside Mount Pleasant, Route 26 intersects with Crum Road, which some felt was a short cut to Walkersville. Parents felt, and they were right, that Crum Road was too narrow, with too many bends and turns for a school bus. Also, at that time, there was an old one-lane bridge on Crum Road. Just before you got to the bridge, the road had an ascending pitch to it, forcing your car to go up and then down pretty fast, giving you that roller coaster feeling, and you were coming down on an old wooden bridge that had seen better days. For safety reasons, bus drivers were told not to use Crum Road. Well, one day, the kids (we're talking 12- to 13-year olds) pleaded with the bus driver to take them to school by using Crum Road. She not only did what they asked, but she also increased her speed just before the bridge, as they were asking her to do. The bus went up in the air and came down with such force that practically every kid on the bus went up in the air with it, causing many kids to hit their heads on the ceiling of the bus, fall into the aisle, and get hurt. None of the injuries was serious, but that was not known until every kid was taken to the hospital and checked.

When I returned from the hospital, I was livid. (Just the previous week, I had reported to the Transportation Department that some parents had called saying that this same bus driver was driving too fast in their development. Transportation officials told the driver about my call-in complaint even before the Crum Road incident.) Many of the kids ended up with an assortment of bumps and bruises. I called Transportation, told them I didn't want that woman driving for me any more, that she should be fired immediately, and that she would be lucky if the parents did not file a legal complaint. They told me they would take care of it. I didn't hear any more from them. The next day we had a new driver.

New Market Middle School opened the following September. On the third day of school, I got a phone call from a parent complaining about a bus going pretty fast in her neighborhood. She didn't know the name of the driver, but she gave me the bus number. When the bus came into school that morning, I was waiting for it. After the kids got off, I stepped on the bus, and I couldn't believe my eyes! It was the same driver who rode over the bridge. I told the driver that she should go home and wait for a call from Transportation, because I was calling them *right now*. Transportation told me that they had suspended her for a time last year and then took her back because drivers were hard to find. I told them that if that driver was on that bus when it came back to school that evening that I would not allow the kids to get on it. And also, I would scream all the way up the ladder about this. She did not come back that evening. Later, I was told that she was given the choice of resigning or being fired.

### What's In A Name?
Evelyn Holman, the director of education, introduced me to the parents. (Charlotte Smith had been abruptly demoted by the then-current

superintendent, which many of my colleagues and I thought was a sad day for education in Frederick County. Charlotte retired soon thereafter, way too soon.) Roy Okan was supervisor of science then, and I remember him making two comments during the evening, one of which did not please "boss" Evelyn. When one of the parents asked how we got into this mess of both Green Valley and Linganore being so overcrowded, Roy's comment was that there were obviously too many rabbits in the area. Evelyn was already on edge because the parents weren't too happy with sending their kids on the long trip to Walkersville on a school bus. Some parents had already been voicing their concerns about whether Walkersville was the best option the school system could come up with. In fact, in a newspaper article that same week of the meeting about this possible move and the parent protest, one lady was quoted as saying that the only reason for the school system to want our kids going to school in Walkersville was because it was convenient for the new principal, Mr. Shade, who happened to live near Walkersville.

The parents didn't laugh at Roy's comment, maybe because of the glare he was getting from Evelyn. Everyone took Roy's second comment of the evening more kindly. The question on the floor concerned what we would call this building for one year. Parents had made it very clear that "the old Walkersville school building" was unacceptable. Roy broke it down very succinctly. He said that because we have only one grade, seventh, we were not a middle school, and certainly not an elementary school. He suggested that we call the school Linganore West since seventh grade at that time was still part of the high school. He also suggested that my title should be associate principal of Linganore High School, answering to George Littrell, principal at Linganore.

Ironically, I never talked to George once during the one-year existence of Linganore West. That is not to imply that there was any animosity between George and me. It was just that he was very busy with his school and I was very busy with mine, in addition to attending progress meetings on New Market Middle and all the other responsibilities associated with that school. The following year the Board of Education decided that principals of brand-new schools would be named one year in advance, like I was, but would have no other responsibilities, other than getting their new school ready to open. This decision didn't help me, but I was happy for all the principals coming after me.

Linganore West existed for only one year, but I loved every minute of it. My days were long; I worked weekends, and by the end of the year, I was physically and emotionally exhausted, but I never once regretted that wonderful year.

Many years later, whenever I would ask anyone from the Board if they had ever heard of Linganore West, the answer was always no. It seems that there is no official record of its one-year-only existence, except maybe on a piece of a dust-, dirt-, and grime-covered paper in the Board basement.

## Working Things Out

During my 28 years as a principal, there were only two grievances filed against me. I did my very best to attempt to work things out before they got to that level. I would ask teachers and/or the Frederick County Teachers Association (FCTA) representative to talk to me first about any problems. The first grievance occurred at Linganore West, and the second occurred a few years later, when I was principal at New Market Elementary.

I was a stickler for wanting staff members to look and dress as professionally as possible. It didn't have to be three-piece suits and neckties, and it didn't have to be dresses and high heels. One of the teachers who was transferred to Linganore West from Linganore High to teach seventh grade had the habit of wearing a tee shirt and either khaki pants or blue jeans. He and I talked several times, and he would tell me every time that as soon as he got some extra money, he was going to buy some suits. I told him that I wasn't interested in suits, but I would like to see him wear, at the least, dressier pants and a collared shirt. I suggested that he wear whatever he would wear to a social or to church or out to a casual dinner. He nodded but didn't respond. A few days later, he came to work in a tee shirt and khaki pants, both items dirty with smudges of grease on them. I asked him to come to my office, and I was direct. I acknowledged to him that I applauded the fact that he was active in FCTA, working hard for higher pay, better working conditions, and for the Board to treat teachers like professionals. And I concluded by saying that if he wanted to be treated like a professional, then he should start dressing like one, not coming to school looking like he just finished changing the oil in his car. He told me he *had* been working on his car that morning before school, but he had not changed the oil. I told him that I was giving him a verbal reprimand by this conversation, and that I would follow it up with a written reprimand if he continued to dress as he did today. He wore "dress" pants and a sport shirt to teach in the next day. (He was a classroom teacher, not a shop teacher.)

The following day I received a call from the teacher representative from FCTA, asking if he could talk to me. Without asking why, I replied yes, because I figured I knew the reason. We talked about the conversations the teacher and I had had about the manner of dress. He was pleasant enough but after about 10 minutes, he banged his fist on the front of my desk, and said in a loud voice: "You have *no right* to tell my teachers how to dress." At that point I wasn't sure if I had the right or not. I was intimidated by his action. But, in my heart, I just knew I couldn't be wrong about this, and I refused to withdraw the verbal reprimand. This part was a good learning tool for me. My heart and/or gut feeling had nothing to do with it. The contract language had everything to do with it. I made a vow to myself that day that never again would I have a conversation about these types of things without knowing how I stood in relation to the teachers' contract. As it turned out, the language was vague, open to different interpretations, depending on your viewpoint. My boss was neither for nor against me; she was interested in effecting some sort of compromise. But I wouldn't budge, and neither would the representative. So, a week later, the teacher was transferred to another school. I saw him a few months later, at a teacher inservice meeting, wearing khaki pants and tee shirt.

## Tough Decisions

I need to talk about the point I raised about my boss appearing to be neither for nor against me. One thing that I did learn as I got older and more experienced was that my perspective about a situation and "downtown's perspective" were sometimes at opposite extremes. I knew that they had to look at "the big picture." And quite often they had far more information and knowledge than I did about things. But, on the other hand, when they interview you and hire you for leadership positions, one of the questions they always ask is, "Can you make tough decisions?"

There are many tough decisions that good administrators make every day. Many decisions aren't the best, but too many times principals find themselves sitting out on a limb by themselves, knowing that they had made a correct decision, while the boss, quite often having heard only the version of a teacher or parent, decides that he or she knows what's best and overrules the decision.

My assistant principal made a good — and correct — decision a few years ago. After my boss heard from the parent involved, she called me to question my assistant's decision. I explained the situation to her and suggested that she didn't quite get all the facts from the parent. The parent wanted her child moved from one teacher to another teacher, even though that would place the child in an incorrect reading group. The parent appealed my assistant's action, and after talking to the parent, I decided that my assistant had made the best decision for the child. The parent told me that she would appeal to my boss, and I told her she had every right to do so. I also, perhaps naively, told her that this was one decision that wouldn't be overturned. (While they were leaving, the father told me that I was underestimating the tenacity of his wife.)

Maybe I could have worded it better, but when I told my boss that possibly she hadn't gotten all the facts, her response was, "Tom, I am your superior, and you will do as I say." And I did. I wrote her a note the next day, not questioning her authority to overrule a decision, but letting her know that in more than 25 years, I could count on one hand how many times I had been told that I did not make a correct decision regarding the best situation for a child. I ended by telling her that I would follow her directive but was disappointed in her lack of trust for, and support of, my assistant and me.

The child was moved to the requested teacher and placed in a reading group that we felt was incorrect. About a month and a half later, the family moved to another county. I received a telephone call from the principal of the new school. He told me that the child's mother had registered her daughter at his school and was insisting on having her daughter placed in a reading group that he and his reading specialist, after testing the child, felt was at a level too high, and too difficult, for the child. Her insistence also came with the statement that the child was in that same reading group at her previous school. I told him that we were directed to make that placement. I don't know where the principal ended up placing the child.

I am absolutely in favor of giving great credence to parents' opinions. They know their children much better than we do. But there are times, and I felt that this was one of them, when the parents should have listened to our advice. Children need challenges, and in many cases they can handle the extra push. In this instance, though, we felt very strongly that being challenged was not the issue. We were certain that this parent was more concerned with having her child with a particular teacher and with particular classmates, than in having the correct reading group placement for the child.

## Unsatisfactory Observations

My other grievance came from a teacher whom I was trying to dismiss as incompetent. After three years of unsatisfactory observations and evaluations from the language arts supervisor and myself, I recommended that we not renew this teacher's contract. After several levels of hearings, with no decision, we ended up downtown with the superintendent, board lawyer, FCTA representative, the teacher, and myself. After hearing discussions from both sides, the superintendent declared that the teacher would keep her job.

Even though there were three years of unsatisfactories, all the unsatisfactory observations took place in language arts class. This was a second-grade teacher, and I believed that language arts/reading was too important an area in which to be found unsatisfactory. Everybody agreed. There was, however, a three-year-old observation in her file that had been marked satisfactory. This observation took place in a math class and was done by my assistant principal. My contention was that this one observation showed that we were being fair to the teacher—that I did not say to my assistant that he should go in her class and mark her unsatisfactory regardless of what he saw. In three years, we found her to be satisfactory in *one* observable situation. The Frederick County Teachers Association representative's contention was that my assistant and I were not together; that we could not agree on whether one of our teachers was unsatisfactory or not.

The superintendent's decision did not bother me. It was fair to the teacher that the superintendent takes everything into consideration. My side should be able to prove without a reasonable doubt that this teacher should be dismissed. I knew the old observation was in the file; I didn't know it would affect the outcome of the hearing. We learned from that, and the only thing to do is move on and vow to do better the next time.

The teacher remained at our school. I could live with that, because that's the way it worked sometimes. But I still felt she was an unsatisfactory teacher, and I had a decision to make. One way was to start the process all over again, continue to work with her and offer help, make my observations, and if she still continued to be considered unsatisfactory, move to dismiss her again. This would take several years.

What bothered me about this was that I knew if we again found her to be satisfactory on another observation that was not done in a language arts class, we would lose again. Not all observations are done in one discipline, nor should they be. She could be observed in science, social studies, or math, in addition to language arts. My contention was that she should not and could not teach reading to young children, because she was not effective or successful in this area. This was the shared opinion of at least four persons who had observed her over the years.

One option was to mark her satisfactory in everything during the next school year and then excess her at the end of the year. (A teacher who had unsatisfactory marks on an observation or on her annual evaluation could not be excessed.) This was the option I chose. I was beginning my fourth year with this teacher. I had provided all the help and advice our system had to give. I had followed all the due process steps to which she was entitled, found her to be unsatisfactory for three years, with the exception of one math observation, and was unsuccessful in getting her dismissed. (This is the same teacher I referred to earlier who told me that her previous principal only excessed her very best teachers from her staff, to which I had replied, "That's b.s. and you know it.") Maybe another principal could help her more than I had.

It was not unusual for some teachers to be moved from one school to another every year or two. A teacher is considered to be tenured at the end of the second year of teaching. After that, it is very difficult to dismiss a teacher for other than extraordinary circumstances.

The vast, vast majority of teachers are very good. But every school administrator gets frustrated over how to resolve the problem of the tenured, but unsatisfactory teacher. When Dr. Stuart Berger was superintendent of our school system, he attended a monthly meeting of school administrators to discuss this very issue. He told us that he was directing his people to make a list of all the teachers who are continually marked unsatisfactory every year, trace those teachers back to the school in which they worked when they were tenured, note the name of the principal of the school in which they were tenured, and transfer those teachers back to the school where that principal was currently working. I applauded that bold comment but that meeting room was as far as it went.

## Overcrowded Before September

New Market Middle School was built for 900 students and opened in 1979 with more than 1,100 students. We were overcrowded before the first day of school. It was decided that roughly 200 sixth- graders would be housed next door at New Market Elementary School. I felt terrible about this, but could come up with nothing better. One of the biggest attractions for sixth-graders coming to the middle school was getting a wall locker. The 200 kids next door would not get one. This was not very popular with the kids or their parents. My boss suggested that I create my reading groups for all sixth-graders and then by random drawing send as many sixth-grade groups next door as it took to reach the number 200. That made sense to me. I completed the groupings, placed them in a hat, and made the random drawings.

My boss called me about a week later and implied that maybe I was a bit too naive to be in charge of this big school. One of the sixth-grade students was the daughter of a Board of Education member, and she happened to be in one of the groups assigned to the elementary building. My boss indicated that a *savvy* principal would have known this before he did the random drawing, and he would have made certain where this student would end up. I was hurt, embarrassed, and confused. I wanted so badly for everything to go well. I knew that we had a board member's daughter, but it just never occurred to me to do what my boss suggested. The student remained at the elementary location.

I committed quite a few of those types of errors during those two years, which didn't endear me to my superiors. Once I wrote a letter to the owner of a large, local newspaper, complaining of his wife's unfair treatment of us. Many, many subcontractors are hired to do certain specific tasks at a new building. In this case, it was the making of nameplates (literally hundreds) for our building. There were nameplates for bathrooms, classrooms, special education rooms, the lounge, the speech classrooms, shop area, and so forth. Every door in the building had a nameplate.

The sub-contractor hung all the plates on the walls. Upon inspection of the plates after the work had been finished, we discovered several that had grammatical errors. The sub was notified and he told me to leave them on the walls and he would make replacements and have them up before school started. In the meantime, the wife of the newspaper owner had requested to use one room in the building for a women's group meeting. The building had been inspected and approved for us to use. This meeting was to take place the week before school started. When she came in with her group, she noticed some of the incorrect nameplates. She didn't say anything to me, and it didn't occur to me to explain about the wrong plates. But apparently, she saw this as a "scoop" for the newspaper. The next day, she sent a photographer from the paper to the school, and he took pictures of the incorrect nameplates. The photographer entered the school without signing in, even though there was a sign in our entrance hall directing all visitors to sign-in before going into the instructional areas of the school. In the next edition of the newspaper, a picture of one of the incorrect name plates appeared along with a caption that questioned how teachers could teach correct grammar and punctuation when they couldn't even get their own signs right.

I was angry. I called her to verify that she had sent the photographer. She confirmed it. Then I told her that she would not be welcome to use our school again, and I wrote her a note to confirm it.

Three days later, my boss called and told me that I had over-reacted and would have to rescind my non-welcome speech. Publicly, I obeyed her directive; privately, I simmered and yearned for school to start so that I could keep busy with kids, teachers, and lunchroom duty.

## Discipline

When our middle school opened, everyone agreed that it would take three to five years to make middle school philosophy become a reality. Part of our problem was that I was an elementary person and came in with an elementary mind-set. The majority of the teachers were transferred from Linganore High School, and they came with a secondary school mind-set. There were some clashes, some agrees-to-disagree, some compromises, and some "we'll do it this way" directives. There were some great teachers who came to the middle school, and I have fond memories of all that we accomplished together.

One of the areas in which the teachers and I disagreed most was discipline. I have always felt that teachers needed to be supported by my assistants and me. And we did the best we could to make that happen. But in a big school, not everyone is going to be consistent about whom they send to the office, for what kinds of infractions, and what kinds of punishment they expect to be handed out. Most teachers took care of smaller, routine things, such as not having a pencil, talking in class, showing up a few minutes late, and so forth. When those teachers sent somebody to the office, I knew that they had exhausted their remedies and were asking for my help, and I gave it to them.

Some teachers sent kids to the office for everything and, after awhile, I would send the kids back with instructions to the teacher to attempt to work it out in the classroom first. Teachers have to be accepted by the kids as the person in control of that classroom. Anything less and the kids will not respect them. Another thing that was unacceptable to some teachers was the punishment. Some would write a referral and at the bottom indicate the consequences to be given to the child. My philosophy — which I shared with the teachers early on — was that if you have run out of things to try next, or even if you haven't tried anything, once you send them to me, I will decide the consequences, if any. More than 95 percent of the referrals sent to the office were legitimate. But I wouldn't do anything until I heard the kids' version of the incident. And sometimes, I sided with the students. Teachers are in charge and deserve the utmost respect from their kids, but they should never allow themselves to get into shouting matches or make threats to kids that they cannot carry out.

I found a note in my mailbox one day. It said, "Dear Tom, if you would spend more time in your office beating the asses of these kids who deserve it, instead of always standing in the hallway, greeting and hugging the kids, this school would be a lot better off." There was no signature. I read it that evening at a staff meeting and asked the teachers if anyone would like to discuss this note. There was no response. I was never angry about that note. I think it was a fair and honest expression, except for the fact that it wasn't signed. It may have represented the feelings of one person or more than one, but I knew we had a lot of work to do.

Middle school kids were everything I expected, and more. They were so full of life, so exciting, so much fun to be around. Boys were very predictable. I knew that they would run, push, argue, cry, laugh too loud, tease, and trip over their own feet. And when I had them one on one, away from the group they were trying to impress, they would listen to reasonable suggestions and, quite often, stay out of trouble, sometimes for a week or more. Girls were not as predictable. Many were more mature than the boys, worked harder, and did not fight like boys, but when they got angry, especially if a boy was involved, it was total war. Most of the boys and girls acted like they were 12 and 13 years old, which I liked. Some of the boys acted like bullies, and some of the girls acted like they were 15 and 16 years old, which I didn't like.

I have told many people that eighth-grade girls caused my premature gray hair. This was not true, of course. If anything, both the boys and girls kept me younger.

## Challenges

Once a student has been coded special education, such as "speech impaired," "learning disabled," or "mentally retarded," to name a few, there are provisions within the special education law that protect the child. And justifiably so.

I remember a seventh-grade boy at New Market Middle School. He was in special education and was coded "emotionally disturbed." I'll call him Phillip. After Phillip was caught smoking in the bathroom a second time, I decided to suspend him from school for three days. His mother objected to the punishment and appealed it to our special education department. Her objection was based on a special education law that states that consequences or punishments may not be given to a student in special education for offenses if said offenses are a result of the student's handicapping condition. His mother claimed that Phillip was coded emotionally disturbed, which caused him to get nervous, and when he got nervous, he smoked, which calmed him down; therefore his smoking was a result of his handicapping condition.

For a multitude of reasons, most of which had nothing to do with special education, I contended that nothing gives a student the right to smoke in school. Our special education department supported my decision to suspend. The mother appealed to a higher level, and a Special Education Advocate Group represented her.

Our board attorney got involved, and for the next several weeks, literally hundreds of documents were copied and shared with both sides. Ultimately, the case went before a hearing officer trained and hired to adjudicate these types of special education issues.

During a break in the hearing, I was out in the hallway, by myself, when Phillip walked toward me. I was upset and nervous about testifying under these conditions, being cross-examined, and having Phillip and his mother's attorney challenge every statement that I made concerning school discipline. Phillip walked closer and said, "Mr. Shade, when this hearing is over, and we win, I am going to come back to school, light up a cigarette, and blow the smoke right in your face." What I whispered back to Phillip should not have been said by a principal to his 15-year-old student. I told Phillip that if he did that, I would take him through the goddamn wall. Phillip just looked at me. I couldn't tell if it was a smirk or a smile. I overreacted to Phillip's comment, and I'd like to think that I wouldn't have followed through with that threat. They lost the case, so it became a moot point.

### "Downtown"

New Market Middle School was the first grade 6- to 8-middle school in Frederick County. Because many people wanted to learn about the philosophy, classes were offered for prospective middle school teachers and administrators.

One of my teachers came into my office one day and asked if I was sharing information with anyone "downtown" about our school. I asked, "What kind of information?" She mentioned nearly all the problems that we'd had with opening the school. When I asked her how she knew about them—I had not told anyone at the school level about some of the situations because some of them were confidential and shouldn't have been shared with others—she told me that she was taking a middle school class being taught by a high-ranking supervisor in the system. She said that at every session, the supervisor would tell of a concern or problem that was occurring at New Market Middle, and the class would discuss the problem and critique the principal's resolution of the problem. When I asked the supervisor why he was doing this (we were in the spring of our first year), his response was that real-life problems were more meaningful, that the discussions were constructive, and I was being too sensitive. When I asked him where he got his information about the "issues" he was discussing, since some were confidential, he wouldn't tell me. I didn't bother asking my "boss" where he got his information because I knew she wouldn't tell me either.

Early in the second year, a parent asked me why I didn't attend the every-other Friday administrator/parents get-together sessions at different parents' houses. I didn't tell her that I didn't know what she was talking about, but instead asked her how they were going. I added that

I had been very busy and I wasn't even sure which of my assistants was attending. She told me which assistant it was, and said that the assistant, along with my "boss," conducted the sessions. The discussions always centered on parent concerns about the school, she said.

At first, my "boss" denied that the meetings were being held, but she later admitted that they were. When I asked her why she felt it necessary not to invite me, her answer was that parents would talk more freely in my absence. I was crushed by their actions.

I had always made it a practice not to take my work problems home with me. But that weekend, I unloaded to my wife, and she did exactly what I wanted her to do—she listened. I had never been a quitter, but this was getting to be more than I could handle. Plus, half my administrative staff was getting direction from another office. On Monday morning, I called my "boss" and told her that I would like to be transferred out of the middle school as soon as possible. She laughed, as if nothing had ever happened, and said to me, "Poor baby, you don't need a transfer, you just need a rest." I repeated my request and hung up.

When my boss did not respond to my request after a few days, I wrote directly to Superintendent Dr. Gordon Anderson, asking that he transfer me immediately. The only explanation I gave was that it was for personal reasons. The next day, my boss showed up with the letter to Dr. Anderson in her hand. She was extremely angry with me and told me that I didn't have direct access to the superintendent; that everything must go through her. I repeated that all I wanted was to leave that school and get out from under her direct control.

At the end of that school year, some eight months after my request, I was transferred to the 160-student Carroll Manor Elementary School. My written request to Dr. Anderson was neither acknowledged nor responded to. And life goes on.

That summer, Dr. Anderson moved on, and Dr. Stuart Berger replaced him. I replaced the highly respected Warren Dorsey at Carroll Manor when Warren decided to retire. My new boss was John Thompson. Three months after I went to Carroll Manor, I received a telephone call from my old middle school boss, asking me if I would go back to Green Valley Elementary School immediately as its principal. When I left Green Valley three years earlier, I had been replaced by my best friend in the education business, Hugh Nolan. Hugh and I were local basketball referees during these years, although Hugh was considered the top-ranked and best official, and I was his occasional partner. We used to joke that our jobs were good training for the abuse we sometimes took from the home crowds at the games. When the telephone call came, Hugh was in the last stages of his battle with cancer. He died a few weeks later, but I declined her request. I just didn't feel it was in my best interests to work for Mrs. Holman anymore.

When I went to Carroll Manor, I went from supervising about 60 teachers to about eight teachers. In the spring of that first year at Carroll Manor, Dr. Berger visited me for the first time. It was a very short visit because he said only two things to me. "One," he said, "you are making too much money to be at a school this small and, two, I am transferring you to New Market Elementary School. If you do a good job, you'll be there three to five years; if you don't, I'll move you out of there immediately." I retired from New Market Elementary 15 years later. Some people didn't like Dr. Berger's directness and tone. If he had concerns about somebody, he would talk to them one on one and not mince words. He reminded me of the story they used to tell about Vince Lombardi, the legendary football coach. When a player was asked one day how he was treated by Coach Lombardi, the player replied, "Coach Lombardi treats us all the same; he treats us all like dogs." Once, I had invited Dr. Berger to a staff meeting at New Market Elementary School. I wanted them to meet him, and I wanted him to address my staff on some educational issues. With them he was absolutely charming, witty, and extremely informative.

When I left New Market Middle, it was with a bitter feeling. I didn't think I was given the time and support needed to finish the job. To this day, I am still confused by the actions of my boss and others "downtown." But, in hindsight, they probably had no choice but to move me. That huge school needed a much more experienced person to open and run it. I think my boss would have had much more confidence in someone who had worked with both elementary and secondary teachers, but I think she compounded some of the problems with her own fair share of mistakes. I never got the staff, including my own administrators, to function as a team, and that was my fault. Looking back on that time, some 20 years later, and with the bitterness gone, I believe I would like to have the chance to do it again, this time with more wisdom and fewer mistakes.

*Let every dawn of morning be to you*
*as the beginning of life, and every*
*setting sun be to you as its close; then let*
*every one of these short lives leave its sure*
*record of some kindly thing done for others,*
*some goodly strength or knowledge*
*gained for yourself.*

John Ruskin

# New Market Elementary School
## 1982 - 1997

Soon after I arrived at New Market Elementary School, an aide at the school, Barbara "Bobby" Garver, approached me. She came in to tell me that she would not continue to work at the school. Not knowing what kind of job Bobby did, I was not too concerned about her leaving. There were many applications from people wanting these 10-month jobs, but I asked why she wouldn't stay. She said it was because of me. She had heard that I got rid of people who didn't do what I said and, also, that I was hard to work for. I chose not to tell her that I had never gotten rid of anybody, but I did tell her that I thought I was pretty easy to work for. I said to her, "Bobby, why don't you stay on for a few weeks, give me a chance, and if you don't like the way things are going, leave then."

Betty Jeffers was a 10-month secretary, had been at NMES for years, and knew every kid, every parent, where they all lived (useful when making transportation bus routes), and everything about the school office. Every administrator learns fast that in order to be successful, you have to work closely with, and have support and loyalty from three groups: the office people, the cafeteria ladies, and the custodians. Betty and Bobby made the minimum of wages, came to work early, stayed late, took work home, and treated parents, teachers, kids, and fellow workers like family. They were superior at their jobs, represented our school in the most professional manner, and most importantly to me, were super, super child advocates. Fifteen years after I went to New Market, the three of us had decided to retire. It was made very clear to all three of us that each deserved, and could have, separate retirement parties. We made it clear that we wanted to go out together, and one party was enough. I considered myself extremely lucky and fortunate to have worked for 15 years alongside these two wonderful women.

Fifteen years is a long time, and I could fill a book with this school alone, so I am just going to pick out and write about some of the incidents that will remain forever in my mind.

## Younger Vs. Older

When I first began hiring teachers, I favored brand-new 22-year-old college graduates. They did not have children yet, and they usually gave 10-12 working hours per day. Women who were in their thirties and forties usually had children in school, were ready to start or restart their careers, and brought a wealth of knowledge, wisdom, and understanding with them, because of their experiences with their own children. Barbara Onofrey was a member of this latter group. I met Barbara when our children swam for the same swim team. In fact, the wife of one of our coaches, Michele Krantz, introduced me to her. Barbara had been working at a local Catholic school, but she had an application on file with our system. She was interviewed, hired, and came to work at New Market.

One day, as she was walking down the hallway, she passed by a second-grade student named Bo. Bo weighed more than 160 pounds, and sometimes his weight and strength got him into trouble, even though Bo wasn't always the instigator. Kids would tease him about his weight; he would lose his temper, and skirmishes would start. Barbara stopped and said to Bo, "Don't I know you? Of course I do, you went to St. John's, where I used to teach. Isn't this amazing, now we are both at New Market." Bo looked at her and said "Yeah, but I bet you didn't get kicked out."

Sometimes principals get a bad rap when they hire teachers just out of college. There are comments such as "he likes to hire the young, pretty girls." Well, more than 90 percent of the new people we hired were young, pretty girls. Mostly, because that's the age when colleges let them go. I hired males every chance I got, but other school systems were offering contracts to them months before they graduated. There are pluses and minuses to the young vs. older, but in my last five to seven years, when I had the opportunity to make my own selections, I chose older.

Somebody asked my wife one day if it didn't bother her that I worked alongside many young, attractive, and single women. Her response was, "If they pay any attention to him at his age, then they have a problem."

## Bat Sickness

I don't remember which year, but the month was October. The kids went home at noon; the teachers were having inservice in the afternoon. Right after the buses left, one of my aides told me that there was a bat outside and it appeared to be sick. I told my custodian to check it out, and he came back later and told me that he had taken care of it. I thought nothing more of it until I received a phone call from the mother of a first-grader who told me that her daughter and some friends were petting a bat at recess and the bat appeared to be sick. I called in the aide, and she told me that 15 or 20 kids had been huddled together by the outside wall of the school, and she thought they were just keeping each other warm like they do on days when the wind is blowing. And yes, it was the area where she later saw the bat. I called the Health Department, and they told me to find the bat and keep it, and they would be out the next morning to help me interview every child on that playground.

The bat was needed to determine if it had rabies. I called in the custodian and asked him where the bat was. He said that he had killed it and threw it in the big dumpster. I told him to get people in that dumpster and find that bat. We had spaghetti, butter bread, fruit, and milk for lunch that day. About 300 kids bought lunch; another 500 brought bag lunches. All the remains and leftovers went in the dumpster. They searched for more than two hours but couldn't find the bat. I climbed into the dumpster and handed out, piece by piece, everything in there. After two more hours, everything was out on the ground, and we still had no bat.

The next day, after interviewing more than 200 first-graders, we determined that 15 students had decided to take care of the sick bat and had touched it often. A letter went home to everyone describing the incident. The Health Officer talked with the parents of the kids who had touched the bat. Because we couldn't find the bat, rabies shots should begin immediately. This was back when a series of shots had to be given over a period of several months. Twelve of the 15 students took the shots; the parents of three refused to allow their children to take them. There are no words to describe the pain, frustration, and sorrow I felt for all those kids and their parents. It was, without a doubt, the most frightening thing that had ever happened in one of my schools.

We had to wait six months, starting with the first shot, to get the "all clear" signal from the Health Department. I can't tell you how relieved I was when that happened. A few weeks after the all-clear, my custodian told me that back on that day, he had indeed killed the bat by hitting it repeatedly with the back of a flat shovel. But instead of throwing it into the dumpster, he had thrown it into the cornfield next to the school. He said he didn't realize how important finding the bat was until I told him about the shots, and then he was too afraid to tell the truth. He told me that he went into the field every day for a week trying to find the bat, but had no success. Then he broke down, cried, and told me that he hadn't slept and that he had lived in horror the past six months, afraid that something would happen to one or more of those kids. He retired soon after that.

## Sweet Tooth
Bobby Garver and I were eating lunch with first-grader Samantha Staub. She had a loose tooth, and you could tell she was having difficulty eating. She chewed on the apple her mother had given her to help loosen the tooth, but got no results. Finally, she gave up on the apple and decided to eat the homemade brownie her mom had baked. One bite into the brownie brought the tooth out. Samantha told us that she was very excited that Mrs. Garver and I were sitting with her when she lost her first tooth.

## The Goldman Group
One summer, I must have received at least a half-dozen phone calls from parents requesting that their child be placed in Stephanie Goldman's group. "Group" means reading placement and also the homeroom classroom. Stephanie was a student in the highest-level reading group in fifth-grade, and her group was full. But one mother persisted. She came in and talked with me for more than 20 minutes. I tried to explain to her that even if Stephanie's group were not full, I still would not put her daughter in it because the two girls were on different reading levels. The mother reminded me that she volunteered a lot, and that she also donated lots of paper to the school from her print shop. I told her that I appreciated that but it would not be fair to her daughter to place her in an incorrect group. The mother looked at me and said, "Mr. Shade, we used to like you."

## Drug Safety
A few years ago, a first-grade teacher was teaching the drug safety unit in the lab, and a first-grade girl told the teacher that her brothers made her do drugs. At first, the teacher didn't believe her, but the student told her that again, and the teacher felt compelled to call the Department of Social Services to file a report of what she had been told.

The rules were adamant then as they continue to be now. If we had any doubt at all, we were to find in favor of protecting the child. The teacher felt uneasy about calling because she knew the family. A representative from Social Services went to the house and upset the mother terribly. She called her husband, who came home from work. He ranted and raved to me about how this would never have happened if the child had been a blond, blue-eyed Caucasian child. (The girl was Asian.) Dad came to the school in a rage, demanded to speak to the teacher, and accused her of racism. I refused to let him speak to the teacher at that moment. I asked him to sit in my office, and I went toward the lunchroom since it was time for the teacher's class to eat. She was heading toward the office. I said to her, "Turn around and walk the other way. The father is here; he wants to see you, and he is mad as hell."

Filing a report with an agency is supposed to be anonymous. It never is when a school files it, because the parents know that that is the only place it could have come from. Administrators and teachers do not make judgments of guilt or innocence. When we have doubt about something, whether it be something we are told or if there are suspicious marks on a child, our rules are very clear. We are obligated to make a report. We are told never to call a parent and make an inquiry first. Even though they have no choice, teachers are always hesitant to report things to the Department of Social Services.

## Hold On To Your Trousers

I told the kids that I would have a tractor race with my assistant principal if they read the required number of hours for National Book Week. They did and I did. The tractors were small lawn mowers. We were to have a foot race to our tractors, start them, and race them to the finish line. To add to the mood, one of the teachers, Joy Milne, brought in two pairs of farmer's overalls. When the starter signaled for the race to begin, both of us ran toward our tractors. Halfway there, the safety pin holding up my shoulder straps broke, and I didn't realize it. Then the overalls fell down to my knees, exposing my underwear. The kids went crazy. While I was looking to a teacher for help, the kids hooted and hollered, and shouted at me to keep running and not stop to pull up my pants. Later, Joy Milne told other teachers that she thought *everyone* knew that farmers always wore another pair of pants beneath their overalls.

## Too Sick To Eat

Notes from home were always appreciated, especially when they were positive. A mother wrote, "I have never forgotten the day that Jo Anna was home sick in first grade. She was too sick to come to school but what really upset her was the thought that this was also the day she was to have lunch with you for getting straight O's on her report card. She asked me to call and let you know that she was sick and you compassionately asked to speak with her. You made that young child feel so special. And yes, you did reschedule the lunch. You probably did that type of thing for lots of children, because I soon learned that is just the person you are. Oh the impression you have made on your students."

I was always surprised when I received a note from parents thanking me for something that I felt was just my way of doing my job. Congratulating kids for exceptional performance on their report cards seemed like a no-brainer to me. I praised them for good work; they felt good about themselves, and they continued to work hard and put forth their best effort.

## Your Slip Is Showing

A first-grade teacher was teaching a lesson about addresses and was being very serious in front of her guests, who were parents and grandparents visiting for National Education Week. The teacher was telling the kids how important it was to know their address. "If you get lost, you need to be able to tell someone your address, or where you live. If you have an emergency at home and have to call 911, you need to be able to tell them your address. Now don't go home and call 911; it's only for emergencies.

"Do you have any questions about the importance of knowing where you live, which we call your address?" Marika stood up, grabbed the hem of her dress, raised her arms straight up over her head, still holding on to the hem, and said, "Mrs. Jubach, I'm wearing a dress today."

## Emergency Cards

At the beginning of a school year, there are dozens of clerical types of things that we require of teachers. One of them is getting students to return emergency cards and getting them to the office. We are lucky if we have 90 percent of them back by Christmas. These cards are important because we need to know if there are any special instructions to follow in the event that school is closed early for some reason. One year, on the fifth day of school, we announced that school would be closing three hours early because of roads flooding from a severe rainstorm. I knew that teachers did not have all their cards back, so I announced for all kids who did not know what they were supposed to do to come to the office. After making dozens of phone calls, we had all the answers. And within a week, I made sure that we had all of our emergency cards turned in.

## Hold My Eye, Please

Ashley was new to our school. She had a prosthetic eye. It was just a few days after school had begun, and we had not yet discussed Ashley's eye with her second- grade classmates. Early in the morning of the second day of school, Ashley put her hand up to her face, "popped" out her eye and sat there holding the eye in her hand. The kids could not have jumped any higher if they had seen a ghost. They rolled, bounced back, and some fell against the wall. The teacher looked at Ashley, then at what was in her hand, and in as calm a voice as possible, said, "Oh, Ashley, we haven't yet told the class about your eye and how it can pop out. Ashley, you should put it back in now so we can talk to the boys and girls about your prosthetic eye."

## Balloons For All

Ramona was a master teacher. She was also one of those first-grade teachers who was a taskmaster and a strict disciplinarian. After adjusting to Ramona's style, parents loved having their children taught by her, but the parents and kids were always just a bit intimidated by Ramona's no-nonsense classroom rules. One day, Ramona was teaching a small reading group at the front of the room. She heard noises, looked up (usually, all it took was a glare), and noticed some boys playing in the back of the room. This never happened in Ramona's class. She walked back, saw that the boys were holding something up to their mouths, and demanded to know what they were doing. Nervously, the boys told her that they were trying to blow up some balloons. Then she noticed. Each of the boys was trying to blow up a condom. In as normal a voice as possible, she asked them where they got their balloons. One boy told her that he took them from his father's dresser drawer. Ramona talked to me, and I told her that I thought the parents ought to know. It was a very embarrassed father who talked to Ramona on the telephone. Both parties agreed that the evidence should be destroyed. Ramona's young teammates were secretly delighted that this happened to Ramona instead of to them.

## Neuter Time

Sometimes, good intentions backfire, especially when you haven't followed the appropriate procedures. There is a Board of Education policy concerning inviting guest speakers into a classroom. Answers that should be known in advance concern what the speaker will be saying and what supplementary materials and/or aids the speaker will be showing to the kids. A short, written form should be filled out in advance, and the principal needs to be notified.

A second-grade teacher learned her lesson the hard way. She had invited a veterinarian to speak to her class. Since the veterinarian was a classroom parent, the teacher didn't feel that she needed to be concerned with following the procedures. The teacher introduced the vet to her class. The vet thanked the teacher and then walked to the front of the class, carrying a bucket. The teacher assumed that the vet would talk about how she helped animals get better when they were sick, and also tell the children some interesting stories. The guest speaker began by telling the class that this was National Neuter Your Pet Month. She continued by telling them about the importance of having their pets fixed. "It's not good," she said, "for your pets to have lots of babies." She removed the towel from the bucket and showed the kids the uterus of a cat and several dead kittens.

The teacher confided to me later that she almost got physically sick herself, not so much from what the vet was doing, but from the fact that she just knew she was going to lose her job when the parents and principal found out what she did. She waited anxiously all weekend for the telephone calls. None came. She admitted to me later that she had learned a very valuable lesson.

## Hall Of Famer

One of our fifth-grade students read an article about the Negro Baseball Leagues. In a report he gave to the class, he told about the living and working conditions of the players. He also related his fascination with the statistics of one of the players, Mr. Leon Day. The student's teacher, Barbara Onofrey, told the class that Leon Day lived in Baltimore. The kids wrote a letter to him and asked about the possibility of his visiting their classroom. He agreed, but when the time came for the visit, he was too sick to travel, and asked his good friend and teammate, Mr. Russell Awkard, to take his place. The kids listened intently to all the stories that Mr. Awkard told. He ended by telling the kids that this was one of the most exciting days in his life, to be invited to a classroom to talk about his experiences as a baseball player in the Negro Baseball Leagues and the segregationist attitude of the times.

Responding to a question from one of the students, he said it was a shame that Leon Day had not been voted into the Old Timers' Hall of Fame, because he certainly deserved it. Leon didn't make it that spring either, but he got in the following year, and our kids are convinced that they made a difference. They had written letters to the Hall of Fame Committee. They got responses back from Roy Campanella, Ted Williams, and Stan Musial, congratulating them for expressing their interest in Leon Day.

## Bet You Can't Catch Me
Fortunately, it was July, with no kids around, when the man parked his truck in front of the school. There were several pigs in the truck. As the man dropped off some papers in the front office, one of the pigs jumped out of the truck and ran into the school through an open door. Donna Kester, one of the school secretaries, saw the pig run down the hallway. Toby, the school custodian, was running right behind it. The pig was snortin' and gruntin' and Toby was chasin' and cussin'. The pig ran into the kitchen and headed for a little storage area that had cubbyholes. Toby pleaded with the pig to come out, but the pig wouldn't move. Eventually, the pig's owner got him out and back on the truck. The man was happy; Donna was still laughing, and Toby was tired.

## Happy Trails To You
On my office wall was a map of the Appalachian Trail. As part of a social studies unit, one of our fifth-grade classes was going to "walk" the trail from Maine to Florida. They measured how far it was to and from their classroom to everywhere they had to travel during a school day, for a whole day, then converted the feet and yards to miles and multiplied the miles by the number of kids in the classroom. That was how far they walked on the trail that day. Each student kept a journal of his or her activities on the trail.

I was walking through the school one day when I heard this shout come from a classroom, "I told you not to eat those berries." In her journal, one girl had written that she had stepped off the trail to rest for a minute and began to eat some berries she saw on a bush. At the end of each day, some kids would come to my office and use a highlighter to mark how far they had walked that day. It took several months to

First-year teacher at Parkway Elementary — 1968

Green Valley Staff - 1973

Tom with the singing Knight Brothers, former students at Green Valley Elementary School (four of the young men still perform together and have appeared in Nashville)

"Conductor Tom" with Assistant Principal Mike Kline during a May Day Celebration at Green Valley Elementary School

Tom with State Senators Ed Thomas (left) and Charlie Smelser (right) at the
dedication of New Market Middle School — September, 1979

Students thank State Senator Ed Thomas for presentation of the
state flag to Linganore West

Having lunch with straight-O students at New Market Elementary

Tom pulls up his overalls at a tractor race while teachers
Carol Beall and Joy Milne help

Tom and Miss Piggy take a bow at Parent Volunteer Appreciation Show

This stubborn pig refuses to walk with Tom during a Children's Book
Week activity — 1995

Tom and students signing to each other

5th Grade Dance

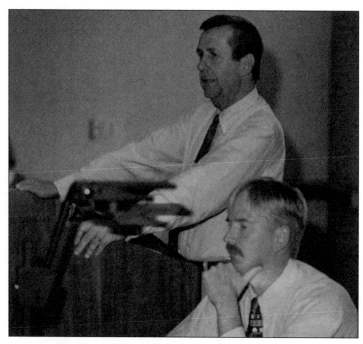

Speaking at an inclusion conference with Steve Parsons, Assistant
Principal of New Market Middle School

Tom with student
Valerie Tressler

Tom with New Market Elementary School Chorus

Tom with 5th grade teachers: (left to right) Ginny Abel, Lauri Gotthelf, Mary Teilking, Missi Motter Snyder, Suzanne Boyle

Playing saxophone while students sing and dance at 5th grade talent show

Mopping the floor during New Market Community Night at McDonalds

Tom with teachers Donna Janc and Janet Manning waiting for Parent Volunteer Appreciation Night show to start

Tom plays piano while teachers sing. Left to right: Sue Abbott, Mary Lee Quealy, Debbie Wills, and Joy Milne

At his 1997 retirement party, Tom is standing with (left to right) sons John and Tom II, and wife Delores

Dr. Jack Dale, Delores Shade, and Tom at
the Maryland Principal of the Year Banquet

Tom with Betty Jeffers and Bobby Garver

Tom/Elvis sings to Ramona Hoth at her retirement party

Tom and teacher Cathy Alspaugh at New Market
Elementary Halloween Parade

Accepting an Academic Achievement Award for New Market Elementary School
with Dr. Jack Dale (left) and Sherry Collette (right)

make the trip. At the end, the kids said that their feet hurt, but they felt it was worth it.

## Purple-Purple

Every school in the system has a sound or code word, known by all employees that would be used in case of emergency. I wanted something out of the ordinary for our code word so I chose "purple-purple."

Quite often, when a child is registered from out of state, the parent informs us that there is a court-mandated custody order and she or he is the primary custodian of the child. And, sometimes, the parent gives us specific directions about who may and may not pick up the child. When this happens, we red flag it in our files and also notify every teacher that the child will have and inform him/her of the situation. One day, Bobby Garver, who was on lunch duty, informed me that a man and woman were walking up and down the hallway, seeming to be looking for someone. I approached them and asked if I could be of any help. They ignored me and kept on walking. I asked them again who they were looking for and the woman told me the name of a first-grade girl who I knew was on our red-flag list. I asked them if they would come to my office where we could talk. (When the father had registered the girl, he indicated that the mother might come looking for her.) The couple ignored my request and started walking toward the first-grade instructional area. I knew then that if they found the girl, they would take her. Our first-grade area was semi-open space and you could see many classes at one time. The classroom the couple wanted was not yet in our view. Before we came close to the room, I yelled, as loud as I could, "Cathy Alspaugh, purple-purple." Cathy was the girl's first-grade teacher, and I knew that she had only one child who had been red-flagged. I just prayed that Cathy knew what I was talking about. We had this emergency code word; the teachers had joked about it, but we had never had to use it.

As soon as Cathy heard me, she knew immediately what was happening. She told the teacher next to her to watch her class, and then she picked up the girl and started running. They went up the back stairs into the fifth-grade area and hid in a supply closet. The man and woman kept walking through the instructional area. I kept yelling "purple-purple" because I didn't want them to know that the child was no longer in that area. After awhile, I steered them back toward the front office. I told the secretary to call the police and tell them it was an emergency. Immediately, the man and woman left.

When the police came, I gave them all the information concerning the child, including where she lived. They left and came back about an hour later and began setting up police teams all around our school. The police told me that the man and woman, who were from Texas, left our school and went to the house where the first-grade girl and her little brother lived. They forced their way in, beat up and tied up the babysitter (who happened to be a retired state policeman), and left with the boy. The police were concerned that they might try one more time for the girl. The father told me later that the woman was the mother of the children, and the man was a private detective she had hired. Assault and battery and kidnapping charges were filed. Soon after, the father withdrew the girl from our school, and we never heard from them again.

### Disruptive Students

Kathy O' Donnell was, without doubt, the best art teacher I had ever worked with. Not just because she was an art teacher, but also because she had so much enthusiasm, so much of a positive attitude. You didn't have to have talent in art to be successful in Kathy's class; if you provided the effort, she guaranteed success.

When I got the message that there was a problem in Kathy's art class, that she needed help, I knew it was serious. When I got there, she told me that Kevin, a fourth-grade boy, had a pair of adult scissors in his hand, had made some threatening gestures, and would not give them up. She had told Kevin that if he did not put the scissors back on her desk where they belonged, she would have to call Mr. Shade. His response was, "If Mr. Shade comes in here, I will punch him in the nose." I walked toward Kevin with one hand extended, and asked him to give me the scissors. He said "No!" Kevin was not a tall boy, and I was kind of stooped over as I got closer to him. I had talked to Kevin many times before and felt that he and I had a pretty good relationship. I had no doubt, as long as I remained calm and Kevin remained calm, that I could get him to hand over the scissors. When I was about a foot away from him, he dropped the scissors, grabbed my necktie with one hand, yanked it down and, with the other hand, punched me right in the nose. I saw stars for a minute or two. Kevin remained standing right where he was. Kathy had gotten the class away prior to this, even though they had seen what he did to me. I regained my thoughts, and calmly asked Kevin to walk to the office with me. He refused and started to dart past me. I reached out, grabbed one of his arms, picked him up and, trying to make sure I didn't hurt him, carried him, struggling, to the office.

When teachers have class sizes of 25 or more, it is very difficult, if not impossible, to deal adequately with these types of emotional disturbances. This was not Kevin's first "physically-out-of-control" incident. There is an alternative program for elementary students with these types of behaviors. There, class sizes are typically not more than one to six, with extra adult help available in the classroom, and a guidance and support component available for the children and their parents. Placement there is not automatic. Regular schools must demonstrate that they have exhausted every strategy and utilized every resource available to them. When you can do that, as we did in Kevin's case, you can have the student accepted into the alternative program.

Usually, when the bizarre behavior results in potential danger to other students and adults, the transfer is immediate. Sometimes, everybody but the parents agree concerning the move to an alternative program. When that happens, the move is on hold until we can convince the parents to agree.

I had another instance of continuous physical outbursts by a child. The necessary documentation for movement to the alternative program was complete, but Mom and Dad would not agree to move their child to this school, which was located outside of their school district. Shortly after our last meeting, the boy became so aggressive and out of control that I called his mother and told her to come get him to take him home for the rest of the day. When Mom arrived, I was alone with the boy in his classroom. (The rest of the class was in music.) Mom walked in just as the boy was telling me how much he hated me. Mom told him to apologize. He screamed at her; she screamed back. He told her that Dad would yell at her that evening for screaming at him. Mom said, "I've had enough," and grabbed his hand to take him out the door. He swung and hit her, and as she fell to the floor, her glasses went flying from her face.

They spent the next two minutes literally rolling on the floor punching at each other. I honestly was not sure what I should do. I wanted to grab the boy off his mother, but because he was being so violent, I was afraid he would get hurt if I had to exert extra force on him, and I would be accused of hurting a child. I thought of pulling the mother away from her son, but felt that solution had an equal chance of going awry. So, I decided to wait them out, watching to make sure that neither of them was in danger of being badly hurt. If it came to that, I knew I would get between the two of them regardless of the consequences. Eventually, the mother got her son around the waist and was holding on for dear life and attempting to drag him out the door. At that point, I tried to grab the boy's legs to keep him from kicking at his mother. He flailed with his hands, trying to knock me back out of the way.

We got him to Mom's pick-up truck. When Mom picked up the cellular phone on the seat to call her husband, the boy swung his fists at her and told her not to call his dad. I grabbed the boy around his midsection, pinning his arms to his side. He screamed and cursed at me. Mom completed her call to Dad, telling him that she needed his help. The boy promised to calm down if Mom would not ask Dad to come to the school. When she finished the call on her cell phone, I asked her if she wanted me to ride home with them. The boy started yelling at his mother again, telling her that Dad was going to be really mad at her. She told me again that she would be all right, and they drove off. It wasn't long after that incident that Mom and Dad agreed to have their child sent to the alternative school.

## Rising Star

A teacher stormed into my office one day, slammed the door shut, and with tears in her eyes, shouted, "Goddamn you, Tom Shade." I said, "Why don't you sit down." With a quivering voice, she replied, "The principal before you thought I was a satisfactory teacher and marked me accordingly on my observations and evaluations. Every time you observe me, you seem to dwell on the things I do well on my observations, and mark me Above Satisfactory. And now I find myself staying up later than I ever did to plan lessons good enough to show you that I am as good as you say I am."

## Bedside Chatter

A woman came into the office one morning, told me she was late for work, and if I wanted her son to come to school, I would have to go get him. She said she was tired of fighting with him every morning trying to get him to school. She told me the front door was open and I would find her son in the bedroom on the right at the top of the stairs. "He'll be under the bed," she said. She and her son lived within a block of the school in a development the kids referred to as "Smurf Village." I walked to the house, opened the front door, and called out his name. There was no answer, so I walked upstairs and knocked on the door of the bedroom on the right. No answer. I walked in, bent over, looked under the bed, and there he was.

He wouldn't come out, so I grabbed his legs and started pulling. He had his hands wrapped around the front legs of the bed so that when I slid him toward me, the bed slid with him. After several tugs and slides, I gave up and sat on the floor. He finally talked. He asked me how long I was going to stay. I told him only until lunchtime because I was on duty today. "Lunch is two hours away," I said. I asked him to tell me about school and especially why he didn't want to go. I told him if he came out from under the bed to talk to me, that I wouldn't force him to do anything he didn't want to do. His problem was something I had expected, and I knew I could and would solve it to his satisfaction. I needed him to trust me and have confidence in me. But, at that moment, he was scared to death.

He was not a big kid. He was slightly built and somewhat shy around his peers. Some bigger kids were picking on him and they had told him he was going to get "beat up" that day. He was terrified. He didn't tell anyone because he said the kids would call him a tattletale and tease him more. I attempted to convince him that I was an expert on bullies. There are three things I would not tolerate: bully behavior and/or making fun of kids; interfering with a child's right to learn; and showing disrespect toward adults or students. I always told the kids who were sitting in my office that, "if both of you weren't laughing, then don't tell me that what you said or did was just a joke."

I told the boy that he could tell me how he wanted me to handle the situation. He could sit in my office as we confronted the other kids together, or I could take care of it myself without the other boys ever knowing how I found out. I told him that in either case, I would guarantee that those boys wouldn't pick him on again. I also told him that there were certain times — and this was one of them — when he had an obligation to report this type of behavior. This was not being a tattletale. Being told that you are going to get beaten up can only be stopped by an adult. He told me that he would be in my office with me when I talked to the boys. We took care of it, and I didn't have to go to his house again to get him to come to school.

## Wacky Ties

My son bought me a tie that looked like a fish. I wore it to school and the kids loved it. After that, somebody was always bringing me some kind of crazy tie, and I would wear it. I was constantly being asked to wear my pig tie, Tasmanian Devil tie, my Where's Waldo tie, or one of my many Disney ties. The neatest part was when a shy second-grader would come up to me, and say, with a big smile, "Mr. Shade, my mommy bought you that tie."

## A Sad Time

Not all the incidents were funny or amusing. One Friday afternoon, I was going over a teacher's observation with him. We were discussing the lesson, all the good things he had done. I ended by thanking him for a good job. He smiled and told me he would see me Monday morning. The next day his wife called and told me he was dead. She told me that he took off in his car on Friday night, and the police called her the next morning and told her that they had found his car and his body. I assumed that he had been in an accident.

After getting over the shock, I called his teammates and arranged to meet them at the school on Sunday, to prepare for Monday, when the kids came back. On Monday, I had many school psychologists on hand to help teachers, parents, and students with their grief. Although I didn't use it often, the handbook for administrators, detailing all the things to consider and do in an emergency situation, was invaluable. At 8:20 on Monday morning, before the kids arrived, I announced over the intercom that we would have a brief staff meeting. Some of the staff did not know of their fellow teacher's death.

One of the psychologists asked me if I would need his help at the meeting. I told him no because I assumed that all the teachers would be buzzing and whispering to each other and also helping to console each other. For my part, I figured I would breeze in, ask them to quiet down for a minute, make my brief statement, and leave. What I got was the last thing I expected. There were more than 65 people in that room when I walked in, and you could hear the proverbial pin drop. The only sounds were those of his teammates, and a few others, sobbing. All of a sudden, I couldn't talk; the words just wouldn't come. I tried to stare over the heads of the people in the rear, but everywhere I looked, all I saw was tears. I lost control of myself. I muttered a few unintelligible words and walked off.

I cannot imagine now how all of us got through that working day. God was certainly steering us. When I left the room, the psychologist was there again, offering me words of encouragement. I don't know if he decided to assign himself to me or not, but I certainly did appreciate his help. I asked him to go with me to the teacher's room. I wanted to be there when the kids came in. I presumed this would be similar to my teachers' meeting, that the kids would be silent and subdued. Wrong. They were standing in small groups talking to each other, many with their parents by their side. It doesn't take long for this kind of thing to spread throughout the neighborhoods. I had to go out into the hallway and ask one kid to go to his seat. He had designated himself to be the person standing in the hallway, announcing to all the kids as they showed up, that their teacher was dead. He was not acting disrespectfully. The kids were all miniature adults. This was a fifth-grade class, so they were old enough to understand what had happened. There was some crying, some shocked looks, but most of the students seemed, at least to me, to be wanting someone to explain all these strange people walking around, all the sad faces, all the commotion. I talked with them and remained with the class the rest of the day. There were many questions, about evenly divided between "why did this happen to our teacher" to questions that started out as questions but ended, as I remember, with comments. We were encouraging kids to talk and share their feelings.

On the previous Thursday, I had held a conference with a parent, who was requesting that I allow her daughter to transfer from this teacher's room to another room. The request was more because of peer relationships than wanting to be removed from that teacher's room. I told the parent that I would arrange it. I talked to the teacher and he told me that it would probably be a good move for the girl. On Thursday evening, I called that parent and told her that we would make the move on Monday morning. After my initial comments on Monday morning to the class, the psychologists took over and did a wonderful job talking to the students. It was suggested that the kids create a corner just for this teacher and place memorabilia there to remind them of him. The teacher was a big man, and he had left a pair of his work boots in the classroom. The size of the teacher's feet had always been a kind of joke that both the teacher and the kids had laughed about a lot. The boots were right in the center of the small monument.

When I finished talking, the girl who was supposed to move to another room that morning asked if she could talk to me. We went into the planning room, and the girl said that she didn't want to move. She started crying heavily and told me that she felt that his death was partly her fault. "He must have been very angry with me when he was told that I wanted to transfer out of his room," she said. I tried to reassure her that he had not been angry with her at all. I couldn't get her to believe that. I took her to one of the psychologists who had more training in these types of things than I did.

The long-term sub I hired was Brian Clopper. He was everything we needed; he had patience, love, understanding, and strength. (In the next few months, he would need that most of all.) He was also a certified teacher who did not yet have a job. I don't think I am violating a confidence when I tell you that he seriously considered dropping teaching as his career choice. Some of the kids were unmercifully mean to him. They would just not accept him as their teacher. And he was also competing with the monument. One day, the dead teacher's wife called and asked if she could come by and pick up his belongings. Once she took his things, including his boots, the atmosphere in the room changed. At least toward Brian.

I hired Brian as a full-time teacher at the end of that year. He asked if he could change grades. He also asked if he could be moved to a separate teaching area. He told me that to teach in that area and at that grade level next year would be very difficult for him. Knowing how hard he worked, and how difficult the past several months had been for him, I had no trouble granting his request. I had a vacancy in fourth grade and 12 portables from which he could choose. Brian became an integral member of our staff.

## Elvis And Ramona

One of our long-time teachers, Ramona Hoth, retired. The staff was having a big picnic in her honor. Elvis was her favorite celebrity, and, before I knew what was happening, Debbie Wills was handing me an Elvis outfit and saying, "Tom, get ready, it's time." There were about 100 people waiting outside for Elvis. In my white rhinestone outfit and wearing a wavy black wig, I strutted out and sang, "Love Me Tender" to Ramona. I looked at Ramona, with her boyfriend, Frank, by her side. She was smiling, just a bit of a tear in one eye. I didn't know if the tear was there because of the beautiful ballad I was singing and that it reminded her of Elvis, or if it was because of what I was doing to her favorite song.

## Grade-A Prime

I had been at New Market several years now, and it had been traditional for the PTA to cook up a steak luncheon for the teachers on their last work day. I was approached by a PTA lady earlier and asked if they could serve cold cuts this year instead of steak. I appreciated all the things the PTA did for us, and whatever they did was great. I was trying to make a joke when I said to her, "This is not a cold-cut faculty; this faculty is prime steak." I thought she would laugh and tell me that she agreed with my analogy, but we were getting cold cuts this year. Well, we did get steak that year and every year after that. I was also never asked again about changing the menu. For many years, Mary Spanberger would bring in the equipment and fix her wonderful onion rings. And, for just as many years, this principal would have to go into the cafeteria early and check out those rings.

## 'Til The Cows Come Home

Missi Motter Snyder was a fifth- grade teacher, and her second-story room looked out over the playground. Adjacent to our playground was a working farm. The only animals on the farm were cows. The fences on the farm were either half way trampled down in spots or had holes in them big enough for a cow to get through. On more than a few occasions, the cows got through the fence and onto our playground. And, on more than a few occasions, I was on the playground trying to get the cows to go back home. Sometimes, the cows and I were more than 30 yards away from where they came through the fence, but I was amazed that once I had them headed in the right direction, they went straight for that one hole they had initially come through.

The kids in Missi's class were used to seeing me chase the cows. And they would let out a roar when I had the cows on the run, seemingly heading for the opening in the fence, and the cows would all of a sudden veer off and head back to the playground. In every instance, the kids would cheer for the cows.

## Kid Talk

Roy Okan, supervisor of science, and I were interviewing teacher candidates one day. He asked his questions and I asked mine. When we were through, he implied that I used unfair interviewing techniques.

When asked why, he said that nuts and bolts questions needed to be asked to find out what the candidates knew and didn't know. I told him that I could teach someone to use a SCIIS science kit, or how to teach a reading lesson, or how to teach division of fractions, but I wanted to listen to them talk about kids, about teaching, and about their goals. I told him that I would know after 10 minutes of listening to them talk about kids whether or not I wanted them at New Market. I used this "gut instinct" method for more than 25 years, and it rarely failed me. I know that Roy felt the same way that I did, but I was still fairly new to administration and interviewing, and I believe that he was just giving me some good advice for future interviews.

## A Conundrum

Carol Stitely was, and still is, a blue-chip kindergarten teacher, but she wouldn't be hired if she were just starting out today. She wouldn't survive the strenuous interviews. A lot of people don't get second chances after a weak interview. If I were going to open a new school today, and I had a choice of kindergarten teachers, I would choose from among Carol Stitely, Michele Krantz, and Lynne Harris, the latter two having taught kindergarten for me at Green Valley. Parents and children absolutely adore Carol. She knew the kindergarten curriculum, worked 10 to 12 hours every day, not counting weekends, and started on July 1 every summer to get her room ready for the coming year.

She was a "10," a master teacher, until the time came for her to be observed. She would sweat; she would get sick; she would panic every time I told her that I would be in her classroom in the next few days for her observation. After a couple years of this, I finally told her that I would no longer give her any advance warning; I would just show up, with clipboard in hand. It wasn't any better for her, but it was quick and less painful.

## The Personal Touch

No matter how many kids we had, I was determined to call each and every one of them by their first names. Even when we went over 1,000 enrollment, I could probably say the first names of more than 950. Kids beam when you call them by name. I would walk up to kids, have them tell me their names, and promise them that I would call them Billy, or Sara, or whatever their name was the next time I saw them. Names such as Teresa or Tammy and a half-dozen others were the hardest because there were so many kids with those names.

If I approached a child and couldn't remember the name, if it was a girl I would deliberately say a boy's name, and if it were a boy, I would say, "Hi Bud." A mother told me one day that her son just loved for me to call him "Bud." Sometimes, they didn't know that I was struggling to remember their name. I talked to kids all the time. I would see a girl in the lunchroom and walk up to her and say, "Honey, your mom called earlier and she wants you to know that she loves you very much." Or, I might say, "Hello, Sweetie Pie, may I call you by your first name, Sweetie, or would you prefer that I call you Miss Pie?" I would try to pick out kids who appeared to be loners, either by their choice or the choice of their peers. Quite often, when I would see them the next day in the lunchroom, they would be having fun with other kids, and someone would usually say, "Mr. Shade, Miss Pie is sitting with us today." And Miss Pie would look very happy with her new friends. Whether it was "Honey, your mom called," or "Miss Pie," all the kids knew I was just joking, and they always went along with it.

Some may feel that this kind of camaraderie was corny, but I feel there was a direct relationship between the way I treated kids and the fact that we had a minimum of vandalism, theft, or other things harmful done to the school. I never hesitated to tell the students that doing something harmful to the school hurt me also. And they didn't want me to hurt. I used to get on the intercom and tell them how proud I was of them and our beautiful school. I would ask them to help me keep our school looking this pretty for their little brothers and sisters and neighbors. I rarely demanded something; I would ask and they would help. And I tried to treat teachers the same way. The kids knew that I loved them, that I enjoyed laughing and talking with them, and they responded by giving me their best efforts.

## Projections And Allocations
By the mid-1990s, we had more than 1,000 kids and 13 portable classrooms outside. Our school capacity was 560. Each school is allocated monies for textbooks, supplies, paper, materials of instruction, and other items. The actual dollar amount is a per-pupil allocation based on the previous spring's estimated projection of enrollment for the school. Next year's staffing allotment was also based on the previous spring's enrollment projection. If projections the previous April indicated that New Market would have 900 students, then I would get operating money for the 900. Staffing is based on one teacher for every 23 students, so I would get 39 teachers allotted

for the next year. Looks good, doesn't it? Not really.

For the last eight years I was at New Market, I got money and staffing based on the previous spring's projections. And for those same eight years, my actual enrollment on September 30 was anywhere from 40 to 60 kids over the projection. I would argue every year with my good friend Ray Barnes, out of whose office these projections came, and with Sherry Collette, director of elementary education, and my immediate boss, that I was always starting school hundreds of dollars short and at least one to two teachers short every year. The answer was the same every year: *all the money had been allocated and there is no more staffing left to give you.* In one of those years, we actually had 70 kids come in over projection. Dave Markoe, assistant superintendent, approved one more position for our school, and he gave me the impression that I should feel badly for the school he took the position from.

Every year, our staffing was not sufficient to cover the current enrollment. We were always asking our teachers to absorb the extra students every September. It was obvious that our system was either coming up with projections they knew were short, or the formula they used was incorrect. My feeling was that it was some of each. I also got the impression from my bosses and from Ray's office that arguing every year about the same thing, which they refused to correct, was tantamount to whining. Whining or not, the important thing was to look at the procedures or formula we were using because if one school, over eight consecutive years, did not have the appropriate staffing or operating budget at the beginning of a school year, then it was time for someone in authority to do something about it.

## A New Chance

I received a telephone call from our Human Relations Department. Would I be interested in having a young person work at my school in the evenings for several hours a day? It would last until she completed the required hours of service. The young lady would work for me, under the direction of the Frederick County Sheriff's Department. She was sentenced by a judge to serve a number of hours, either in custody or in the community under their Alternative Sentencing Program. She was convicted of assault and battery on another young person. I needed custodial help in the evenings, so I accepted the offer. She was a good worker and when her "time" was up, I hired her to work for me as a part-time custodian in the evenings. She did this for several years. During this time, she asked a lot of questions of teachers about teaching. Eventually, she went to college and took teacher education courses. She had been guilty of a youthful indiscretion, served her time, and was now pursuing a good career path. I admired her for her courage and strength.

## Operation Alert

It was early August, and again our school's enrollment had exceeded the previous spring's projection. There were no teachers left on the excess lists nor were there any on the returning-from-leave lists, so I was pretty excited when I was told that we would get an additional teacher. This was strange because normally my boss would wait until the actual September enrollments were in before making any decisions on who would get additional staffing. I was optimistic that I would get to interview and select a candidate of my choosing. A telephone call to my boss quickly confirmed that I would not be interviewing anyone. She said that they would be placing a teacher in my school. I asked why and she responded by simply telling me the name of the teacher being sent to us. Then I knew why. This teacher had been charged with several counts of sexual child molestation at his previous school, had been found not guilty, and needed to be placed in a teaching position in a different school. I was not told anything except that he was assigned to my school. I knew a little bit because I had read about the case in the local newspaper. I wasn't overly concerned about the placement because the teacher had been acquitted, was entitled to return to teaching, and we were selected as his starting-over place. Nevertheless, I wasn't that excited either, and I secretly hoped that none of my parents would get too upset with the placement. Not true. As soon as they heard where he had been transferred, three parents called and asked if the name of the teacher on their child's homeroom list was the same person who had just been charged with child molestation. I said yes and all three immediately asked to have their children taken out of his room. I told them that he had been found innocent in court and I would really appreciate it if they would not insist that their children be moved to another class. I knew that if I removed those three children that more parents would call demanding that their children be moved also. I assured them that I would be vigilant and alert and asked them to support me in this situation. All three agreed to leave their children there. If they had refused my request, I would have kept the children in that classroom, forcing the parents to decide what to do next. Fortunately, it didn't come to that.

Actually, the parents felt the same way that I did; they were just uncomfortable with the whole situation. They felt that if he had been taken to court on these types of charges, then he must be guilty of something. I knew what I had promised the parents, but I also knew that I just couldn't stand outside of his room all day. Also, he had the right to expect me to support him as one of my classroom teachers. I was fair to him and acknowledged his good teaching on his observation reports. But it was the first time in my career that I chose to maintain a "professional relationship only" with a teacher of mine. I wasn't upset with my superiors because I knew that they had no choice but to re-assign him after the verdict. When he arrived at our school for the first time, I invited him to come to my office. We made small talk as I was waiting for him to tell me a little about what was going on in his life. I wasn't looking for a pronouncement of guilt or innocence, but I felt we should be upfront and honest with each other. When he didn't bring it up, I did. I told him that I knew what had been printed in the newspaper, that he had been found innocent, and that my expectations of him were that he be the best teacher he was capable of being. His only reply to me was that he was aware of what other people's perceptions would be concerning him, but that he could not control what others would think. He worked hard; his teammates liked him, and I received only two telephone calls from parents that year, and both of them concerned his very rigid classroom rules. I walked by his classroom every day, as I did every teacher's classroom. This has always been a good practice for school administrators. Being visible to students prevents misbehavior. He transferred to another school at the end of that school year

Several months passed before I heard of him again. The account in the newspaper stated that he had been in his new school on a weekend, working at a computer, apparently looking at pornographic materials. When he left the school that day, he had not cleared from the computer the materials he had been looking at. When a teacher turned on the computer on Monday morning, she found the pornographic literature still on the screen. Several people saw him working at that computer in the building that weekend. A few weeks later, I received a telephone call from the board of education attorney, asking me if I could recall any suspicious incidents involving this particular teacher during the previous year when he worked for me. I told him that, to my knowledge, there were no incidents.

Apparently, there was enough evidence this time to find him guilty of something. I don't know whether the teacher was fired or forced to resign. I do remember reading that he was required to sign a document that stated that he would never again apply for a teaching job.

## Joys Of Driving A Bus

Bus drivers have one of the toughest, and maybe one of the most under-appreciated jobs in the system. They hear criticism from parents, students, teachers, administrators, and supervisors in their own department. Sometimes, the criticism is warranted; other times, they just happen to be there when anger is vented.

A driver's route is set up to provide efficiency. The route is timed in advance so that when parents ask what time the bus will be at their stop, we can tell them, give or take a minute or two. They don't stop at each and every house. It is spread out so that they might stop at a mid-point for a dozen houses. We tell parents that the bus will be at their stop, give or take just a few minutes, at a certain time, so that parents know when to tell their children to head for the bus stop. If every child waits inside his or her house until he sees the bus and then starts to grab his coat, lunch, and books, then this puts the bus way behind schedule.

Grace Rice had driven a bus forever. Grace schedules seat assignments for her kids on the first day of school. This is not popular with the children. Grace is firm; she is consistent; and she will not change her style. This created a problem for us in the evenings. Grace stood in the aisle of her bus every evening, with her list in her hand and directed each and every student to his or her seat. When you are on bus duty, this seems to take forever. Other buses, which came in after Grace, were loaded and waiting for Grace to pull out. Thus, we had a huge backup. Out of respect for Grace's long record of outstanding driving, I would not put pressure on her to hurry up. When Grace's bus was the first in line in the evening, we had the second bus and others that came after that load their buses 10 or 15 yards behind Grace's so that we could direct them around Grace. If Grace knew we had a plan specifically designed for her, she never let on.

One evening, after another bus driver had let out her last student, she noticed that a parent was walking toward her bus, beckoning her to wait a minute before pulling out. The driver opened the bus door but the parent chose to remain in the road, with one foot propped up on the first step of the bus. Words were exchanged. Tempers flared. The bus driver told the parent that she did not want to talk any more about the situation. The parent did not leave, still having one foot propped in the bus. The bus driver closed the door on the woman's foot and started driving off. The woman was hopping down the road on one foot, while the other was stuck in the door. The driver drove about 15 yards and then stopped the bus.

The woman took her foot out from the now-open door and limped to her car. She called me and told me the story, and because of the seriousness of this situation, I referred her to the Supervisor of Transportation. Regardless of who was right or wrong in this instance, I always felt that bus drivers did not get enough training on how to deal with, and/or react to, difficult situations.

### Pot Shots
I was called to the school one Sunday evening by our custodian, who was checking out the school as we did on Saturday and Sunday every weekend. A teacher's windows had been "shot out" with some type of gun. I filed a police report, we got the window replaced, and I assumed it was a one-time thing, possibly some kids fooling around with a gun. The policeman assumed that also.

The next evening, Margie Roames, a first-grade teacher, had worked late and left school to go to her car about 6:30 p.m. Her car windows had been shot at. Another police report. Two more times during that week, a teacher's car windows were shot at. Except for the weekend classroom windows, the other shots seemed to come between 4 and 5 p.m. Teachers had already been alerted to watch out for anything suspicious. I also told them not to remain after school any longer than necessary.

While talking to the policeman outside one evening, we became pretty convinced that we knew where the shots were coming from. There were some trailers on the grounds right next to our parking lot, and the angle of the shots appeared to point to that direction. I asked for permission to call the principal of the middle school next door to us and ask her to make an announcement to all her students requesting information from anyone who might know something about these shootings. A reward was offered for information leading to the arrest and conviction of the offender. Within hours, the middle school principal had students who wanted to talk to me. Only one student had information that sounded promising. I asked the policeman to take over at that point. The student told the policeman that she had overheard a conversation just that morning between two kids who were bragging and laughing about shooting out car windows. She thought the boys were just fooling around, so she thought nothing more about it until she heard the announcement from her principal.

I have learned over the years that once the police or protective services — a division of the County Department of Social Services — take over on a case, that we are no longer in the communication loop. I guess I can understand this, but, especially when we file a report with protective services, there are times when it would help to know what happened. We are required by law to report anything suspicious, and protective services will do the investigation. Even though the person making the report is promised a certain amount of anonymity, it doesn't require a world of smarts for parents to know where the report has come from. And the parents do call, quite often confronting teachers, who are in the position of making most of the referrals.

We suspected that a student who lived adjacent to the school was doing the shooting. We were never told, by either protective services or the police, if they determined who did the shooting. Soon after the middle school student talked to me and I reported that information to police, the shooting stopped.

## Accomodating Others—Or Not

Homerooms usually consist of two to three language arts or reading groups. When you have a large school, as we did, there are sometimes five or six teachers at each grade level. We had more flexibility with grouping kids and assigning teachers than smaller schools had, because we had 12 to 15 reading groups to work with. Many instructional supervisors recommend that principals not allow parents to request certain teachers, and I am sure there are good reasons for that. I never advertised it, but when I got such a request, I would tell parents to put it in writing and send it to me. I also told them that I must have the request before we made our assignments for the next school year. I would not grant a request to put a child in a room that would not have the appropriate reading group for that child. I usually received no more than 10 to 12 requests a year, and considering that we had a thousand students, this was not an uncomfortable number to work with. Besides, I was going to attempt to make 12 parents happier than they would have been. I was never the type of principal who said, "This is my school, we'll do it my way." I didn't have trouble making decisions, but if I could accommodate some parents' requests without compromising our academic program, that was all right with me. I preferred to do it that way. I was never comfortable with power plays. I have defused many parent conferences by stating at the beginning, "Folks, I think I've made a mistake; let's talk about this." Whether or not I agreed with that comment was irrelevant; the important thing to me was not to let something rather small become bigger and confrontational.

I handled discipline situations in a similar way. Anytime I had an incident that required major consequences, I never implemented them until I had a chance to talk with one or both of the parents. It was important that they hear from me everything I knew or was told, how I responded to what was said and how I reached my conclusions, before they greeted a very emotional child that evening and heard the story for the first time from the child's viewpoint. I have learned over the years, both from my students and from my own children, that children will tell only as much of the story as they feel needs to be told to put themselves in the best possible light. I always asked the parents for their help, input, and suggestions.

The vast majority of the time, the parents and I agreed to a consequence before I called the child back to my office to tell him/her of my decision. I would also tell the child that I had talked to his parents. Depending on how serious the incident was, quite often I would ask the child to remain in my office while I talked with the parents. I would tell the parent on the telephone that her child was sitting in the room with me so that both the parent and the child could hear me tell the story. When this happened, I would always assume a business tone, nothing emotional or dramatic. At different parts of my conversation, I would hold the phone out, ask the child if I was telling the story as we both heard it, and the parent would hear the child reply in the affirmative. Parents seemed to like this approach. I received many thank-you notes complimenting me on the sensitive and caring way I handled the incidents regarding their children.

## Bits And Pieces

It doesn't always go smoothly. A boy was sent to my office. I read the referral form written by the teacher. I talked to the child and got his version of the incident, and then I made a mistake. I told the boy to sit in my office while I went to another office to call his mother. I came back about 10 minutes later and couldn't find the referral. I looked everywhere. I just couldn't imagine what I had done with it. Even the boy was helping me look for it. I thought I was going senile because I *knew* that form was on my desk when I left the room. Then I looked at the floor where the boy had been sitting and noticed a fragment of paper the same color as the referral form. I told the boy to stand. Then I told him he had one minute to produce that form, "or else!" (Principals say "or else" a lot, although sometimes we're not sure what "or else" implies.) He unbuckled his belt so that his pants were loose at the waist. Then he reached inside his pants and started pulling out torn-up pieces of the referral form. He had torn up the form and hidden the pieces in his underwear.

## I've Got Your Number

We enrolled a second grade boy. During registration, his mother told us that he had had several operations and several blood transfusions. He got along well with his classmates until one day something or someone upset him. He began yelling and throwing things at the other students. The teacher sent for me. I was not successful in getting the boy to stop crying. I put my hand on his arm to help guide him from the room. He resisted. While I was talking to him calmly, asking him to try to relax, his teacher asked him to go with me to the office. He took one step and I thought that meant that he was agreeing to go. When I put my arm around his shoulder to console him, he leaned down and bit me on the arm, drawing blood. Eventually, I got him to walk to the office where he did calm down. Our school nurse saw that I was bleeding, and, knowing what Mom told us about the blood transfusions, insisted that I go the county Health Department to get a hepatitis B shot. I was sitting in the office of the nurse in charge; she had given me the first shot, told me that there would be two more shots over the next several months, and suggested that I give permission for HIV testing. She told me that the test would be analyzed and the results would be back in about a week. I think she sensed that I was nervous and uncertain about agreeing to HIV testing. I told her that people's perceptions about why someone submits to HIV testing is sometimes quite different from the actual reasons. She stated that everything would be done by using a number system. My identity would remain anonymous throughout the whole procedure because only she and I would know who belonged to my number. I was told to come back in about a week, give my number to a clerk in the office, and I would be given my test results. I went back a week later and was waiting along with some other people for my turn to give my identification number. When my turn came, I told the lady my number and she said, "Yes, Mr. Shade, I have your information right here." I registered a protest with the head of the Health Department, but that's as far as it went.

## Money Matters

A bus driver came in one morning with a student. She told me that on her high school run (bus drivers usually made two runs, the first one to the middle or high school, and the second one to the elementary school), a high school girl told her as she got off the bus that she was missing a $50 bill. The driver didn't have a chance to search the bus between runs. At the end of the elementary run, an elementary child told the driver that a boy was waving money around on the bus. Remembering the high school student, she questioned the boy, but he denied finding any money. She brought him to me and told me that it was my job to straighten this out.

I talked with the boy for 20 minutes, and he told the same story. And I was not going to punish someone for something I couldn't prove. In fact, I was convinced he was innocent. I just sat and stared at him for about 20 seconds. (Actually, I was just trying to think of something else to say.) My staring must have made him nervous because all of a sudden he said, "You can talk to my sister; she'll tell you that nobody saw me find any money." While that was certainly not enough to convict, there was something about the way he said it that made me suspicious.

Well, I decided to try it again. I looked at him and asked him if he believed in magic. He said no. I said, "Well I do, and I am going to turn my chair around and count to 30. When I turn back around, I expect to see that the $50 bill has magically appeared on my desk, *or else*. When I finished counting, I turned around, and the $50 bill was on the desk. The boy was tying his shoestrings.

The boy was new to our school. I called his father and told him what happened. The father told me that he was proud of his son for producing the money, because one year ago, he would not have admitted to it under any circumstances. Then he chastised me for tricking his son. While I admit that I did attempt to trick him, I felt that I had a responsibility to the high school girl to try to get her money back. I called the bus driver, told her that I had the money, and asked for the name of the girl so that I could call her parents. The driver told me that the name of the girl was confidential and refused to give it to me. I told her that when she changed her mind, she could come get the money to return to the student. She hung up.

I wanted to call the parents and ask them to talk to their daughter about bringing that much money to school. An hour later, the bus driver showed up. She told me that she still felt that the name of the child was none of my business but would give it to me in order to get the bill back. I called the mother while the driver was sitting in my office. She told me that she absolutely agreed with me that that was way too much money for a child to take to school. She thanked me and we hung up. The driver was still angry with me. I asked her to sign a receipt indicating that I had returned a $50 bill to her. She signed it, and without another word, walked out.

## Podunk, USA

A family from Chicago moved into our area. They registered two boys, a first-grader and a third-grader. They were great kids, very polite and very well dressed. Within the first two weeks, the first-grader went home twice with muddy pants. He also skinned his knee the second time. When first- graders play at recess, they run, scream, chase, laugh, and play tag with each other. Our students had a lot of fun, and we did our very best to make sure that the kids did not hurt themselves or hurt others while playing.

The mother called me after the first incident of muddy pants and screamed at me. She said that if I couldn't control the behavior of those "bullies" at recess, then I should be replaced. Even though it wasn't pleasant to be screamed at, I take all calls from parents very seriously. I asked my people on recess duty to watch these first-graders carefully to be sure that the games they were playing were safe, and, if needed, stop them from playing "chase me"-type games.

Those on duty reported to me everyday that the kids were playing normal games for their age group and that there was no roughhousing. Well, the next day, an aide came in to tell me that I would probably hear from Mom because the new boy had scraped his knee. She said he was laughing and playing when a girl dared him to chase her, and when he did, he tripped and fell and skinned his knee. The aide also told me that there was nothing anyone could have done to prevent the incident, because it was simply spontaneous.

I was hoping that Mom would hear the story that way from her son and would not get too upset. The next day, Mom came in with Dad. She spent at least five minutes yelling and screaming at me. In fact, at one point, my secretary, Debbie Wachter, called in to ask if I needed any help. I said no. Mom called my first-grade boys an organized gang of hoodlums. (She didn't mention the girls, even though I knew that she knew that all the boys and girls played together.) She told me that from now on she would be at every recess, catch the perpetrators (her word), and hand out punishment on the spot, since I wasn't capable of controlling things. I told her that wouldn't be permitted and that I would double the number of people on the playground to ensure the safety of her child. She started screaming and yelling at me again. When they had registered their children, her husband had introduced himself to me as "Sal." I turned my chair to him and said, "Sal, what do you think?" She stood up, pointed her finger at me, and said, "Don't you dare call him Sal; he is Dr. Butler to you, and you call him that."

By this time I was getting irritated, and said again, "Sal, what do you think?" At this point, she stood up, pushed her chair back, and said, "Let's get out of here." On her way out through the office, where people were working and parents were standing, she turned, pointed at me, and said, "Your boss will hear from me. I tried to tell Sal that he was being transferred to the sticks, and that we were moving to Podunk, USA." A few weeks later, they moved back to Chicago.

I wasn't totally sure what "podunk" meant, even though I could make a good guess. So I looked it up and found out that podunk meant "small, anonymous, and inconsequential." I can't honestly say that I was unhappy to see her leave our small, anonymous, and inconsequential school and town. There were several parents, as well as secretaries and aides, in the office when the "podunk" comment was made. It didn't take long for the comment to spread throughout the community and the school. Everybody who talked to my teachers or me about the comment took it in good humor. The comment, though, became a classic. All of a sudden, everyone was proud to be associated with Podunk, USA.

## Tipping The Scales

I loved working with teachers. They were so funny, so serious, so fragile, so strong, and so human. At almost every school I worked in, it was inevitable that someone would start up the "Let's weigh in every Monday morning and keep track of our weight." The funniest incident I ever saw regarding these weigh-ins was at Green Valley. The teachers took these weigh-ins very seriously. If you lost weight from the previous week, you got to wear a cutesy Bambi paper cutout. If you gained weight, you wore a pig cutout for the day.

The teachers would take off everything they could get away with before weighing in. One Monday morning, Florence Awkard took off her shoes, her earrings—everything she could take off—and then stepped on the scales. She was wearing a beautiful, black dress, and all down the front of it was the powdered sugar from the donut she had just eaten.

## Acts Of Kindness

In order to get kids to think kind thoughts and do kind things for each other, we started a Random Acts of Kindness Program. Anyone who caught someone doing a random act of kindness was encouraged to report that act on a form we made—usually, it was adults nominating students—and I would read them each day over the school intercom. Right about the same time we were starting this, I received a phone call from Jose Salaverri. He and his wife, Pat, owned Mealey's Restaurant in New Market and they wanted to talk to me. Jose told me that Mealey's had great success and support in the New Market community and they wanted to give something back, and they wanted to start with our school. I immediately told them about our Random Acts program and suggested that maybe, once a month, we could have a drawing from those Random Acts nominations and award someone a free meal from Mealey's. Pat Salaverri said, "No, let's make it every week, and the winner could also invite a special guest to eat with him or her, on the house." And Jose added, "And let's also draw a name once a week from the list of those people who nominated someone, to receive a free meal." Every week, wow!

So many of the kids nominated were kids who usually never drew attention to themselves, kids who were naturally shy, kids whose home conditions weren't the greatest, but these were kids who were being raised to grow up doing random acts of kindness, whether it was noticed or not.

Two times during the year, I was invited as the special guest to eat with the winner at Mealey's. It was a wonderful gesture from those two kids, and I was just as excited as they were. Not only did Mealey's give hundreds of meals to our students, their guests, and our nominators that year, but also when they arrived for dinner, Jose and Pat greeted and treated them like royalty. Jose made sure that all the other diners in the restaurant that night knew who his guests were and what they had done to get there.

There was an interesting parallel to the nominations.

Teachers had little problem distinguishing between true acts of kindness and those that appeared to be somewhat lacking in sincerity. A third-grade boy began sitting with me regularly at lunch during this time. He was a sharp kid, and I knew he was keenly interested in the program. As we ate our lunch, he said, "Mr. Shade, you know that girl who was nominated today for the random acts of kindness?" I replied yes. He said, "I sit next to her every day in class. Are you sure you had the right person?" A few days later, the same boy sat next to me at lunch. He said, "Mr. Shade, the random acts of kindness thing is going pretty good, isn't it?" I said yes. He waited awhile, then said, "This morning, I picked up a pencil from the floor and gave it back to Melissa." I looked at him and asked him why he was telling me that. He looked me straight in the eye, as serious as he could be, and said, "Just think about it." The next day, when he sat down, I said, "Jamie, I don't nominate people for the kindness program because I'm the one who conducts the drawing each week for the winners, and it wouldn't be fair for me to have my name in the hat and maybe draw it out." He didn't sit with me again for a while.

Winning the meal was fun, but there were other gains. Children seemed to be going out of their way to do acts of kindness. To some, it was something they were learning to do; for others, it was just a natural extension of their normal behavior. Teachers and aides became very excited and did not hesitate to "write up" all the kindness acts they were seeing. It was a great time for all of us. The following year, our system formally adopted the Character Counts! Program. At New Market, we were ahead of the game. Although some kids still occasionally said something mean to other students, many children were displaying more empathy and understanding toward each other.

## Sex Ed.

It was more than a regular workday for me. I was more nervous than usual. I don't know why, because I had been teaching this unit every year, for more than 10 years. I knew my students were anxious for class to start because I had noticed the buzzing and the whispers at lunchtime from both the boys and girls. Today was the day the boys and girls would be separated, and in their respective rooms they would watch the Family Life videos. Some referred to it as the Sex Ed. class. I don't know why because, at our grade level, there was no discussion or viewing of anything representing reproduction.

I totally enjoyed being in the same room every year with all the fifth-grade boys. What they saw were videos, with men and women discussing the growth process of boys and girls, although in later years, the boys only saw the boy video and the girls only saw the girl video. Most of the boys stared straight ahead while watching the video. There was some nervous laughter when male and female sketches were shown, representing various stages of puberty. When the films were over, we had a question-and-answer session. Every year, at least one boy asked a question to test my shock system. And every year, I answered it the same way. "I am allowed to discuss the video and the booklet. Any questions which go beyond that should be discussed with your parents." Actually, the boys, for the most part, asked questions that most boys are curious about. And I can tell you that the vast majority of them definitely were not interested in asking questions dealing with the growth and development of girls. They mostly asked about their own growth and their own bodies, and they were fascinated about how twins and triplets get born.

I always felt good after this session, mostly because the boys saw me in a different light. They knew that I was just as nervous as they were. When they asked something, they would use slang terminology or words they had heard others say. I would direct them to the book and explain that all these words had a more appropriate and accepted term attached to them. And I would end the session with a threat. I absolutely forbade them to talk, discuss, or bring up any topic we had covered that day with any of the girls. "You will not embarrass the girls," I said. Every year, as both groups finished, we let the kids go outside to run off some steam. And every year, a boy would come running up to me and tell me that "the boys keep telling the girls that they are not allowed to talk about the videos, but the girls keep talking about them. Why don't you threaten them?" Every year, I would go to Missi Motter and complain to her that her girls were embarrassing my boys. She would just smile.

## Lost And Found

On the occasions that something had been lost and I was pretty sure that it had been found already by someone else, I used a technique that rarely failed me. I would get on the intercom and say, "Boys and girls, I need your help. So and so can't find the new jacket that his Mom bought for him. I have looked for it and I can't find it either. I know you wouldn't want to go home and have to tell your mom and dad that your new jacket is gone. If you saw it, or found it and forgot about it, would you come to the office now so that we both can thank you." More than 90 percent of the time, a child would show up with the item. I would never question him/her about how or where he found it. I would just thank him. Does this kind of recognition, when you're pretty sure that the kid had the jacket tucked in his backpack, cause the child to take things again? Maybe. I don't know all the answers as to why children and adults do some things. If I did, I wouldn't be writing about all the mistakes I have made over the years.

## Mistaken Identity

Dr. Noel Farmer was the superintendent of schools. At a meeting of our PTA executive committee, I casually announced, "Oh, by the way, I have invited Noel Farmer to speak at the next PTA meeting." As is always the case, the PTA secretary was frantically listening and taking notes at the same time. When the night of the PTA meeting came, Dr. Farmer was sitting in the front row, waiting to talk. The president of the PTA asked the secretary to read the minutes of the last executive committee meeting. She stood and said, "Mr. Shade has invited an old farmer to speak at the next PTA meeting." The normally stoic Dr. Farmer practically fell off his chair. The normal Sphinx-faced expression of this principal turned bright red.

## Hare Today, Gone Tomorrow

A girl told me that she got a rabbit for her birthday and she named the rabbit Mr. Shade. I told her I was very honored and she beamed. A week later, she came into my office and I could tell she had been crying. "Mr. Shade," she sobbed, "Mr. Shade died last night."

## Rhyme Time

I love to talk to kids. They are so exciting, so fresh, so full of life, and they always say what's on their minds. So I guess it was no surprise to me that when I tried to write some poetry, I wrote from a child's viewpoint.

Every year at Christmas, usually the last day before the break, we would have a special morning program that would be televised from the media center, and the kids would watch the program on the television sets in their classrooms. Ceil Lyons was my media specialist/librarian. She mentioned to me a few weeks before the program that she heard that I had written some poetry and would I like to recite some at our morning Christmas program? There would be skits, singing by our school chorus, and many classes singing their favorite songs. I said sure. When it was my turn on the program, Betty Jeffers, the moderator of the program, announced me. I thanked her and told the audience I would like to recite two poems I had written. (Actually, I was very nervous; I didn't really have an audience; I was looking directly at Ceil, who was working the camera and giving me all kinds of hand-signal directions.) I got through the first one okay, but about halfway through the second poem, I glanced at Ceil and the tears were just flowing from her eyes. That rattled me, and I finished the poem by looking everywhere but at her. The first poem was:

### A LITTLE CHILD'S CHRISTMAS PRAYER

*Dear God, I wrote a note to Santa today, but I don't know what to do. The reason I feel that way, dear God, I don't know who to send it to.*

*My brother told me the other day that Santa was make-believe. He said that Santa was for kids my age, and I am only three.*

*But if this is true, dear God, that Santa is make-believe, then who brings my presents, fills my stocking, and decorates my tree?*

*My mommy told me once that if ever I were blue, to go sit down by myself, and have a talk with you.*

*I'm glad I did, dear God, 'cause you'll know what to do, if Santa doesn't receive my letter, see that it's answered, will you?*

*One more thing, dear God, that I would like to say. In case I forget from now 'till then, I wish you a happy birthday.*

And the second poem was:

### A MERRY CHRISTMAS

*Hot diggety! Hot dog,*
*Just three more days to Christmas.*
*Gee, I hope my mommy was wrong*
*About one train for the six of us.*
*But won't they all be happy with me,*
*'Cause after all, I'm just a kid.*
*I got presents for all of us.*
*I did! I did! I did!*
*It all happened the other night,*
*The night I couldn't sleep;*
*I heard my mommy talking,*
*So I quietly went over and peeked.*
*Inch by inch, I opened the door,*
*And very much to my surprise,*
*I saw my mommy*
*With tears in her eyes.*
*And Daddy, too, was standing there,*
*Looking unhappy and very sad.*
*With Christmas only a week away,*
*They should've been very glad.*
*Then my daddy started to limp,*
*And this made my mommy sob.*
*My daddy hurt his legs today,*
*And for this, he lost his job.*
*We must get them something, he said,*
*Something big but something plain.*
*For five dollars, she said,*
*I know where there's a six-piece train.*
*This was all that I could stand;*
*It caught me completely unaware.*
*Slowly, I walked toward my bed,*
*And for hours, I sobbed and stared.*
*The next morning, while walking alone,*

*I passed by Mrs. Bell.*
*Do a couple of jobs, she said,*
*And I'll reward you well.*
*I raked the leaves, washed the windows,*
*Cleaned the branches from 'round the tree.*
*Then I heard, come get your pay,*
*But I stood aghast, all this for me!*
*Four sons Mrs. Bell had raised,*
*And they all had left to marry.*
*She wanted to know if this box of toys*
*Was too much for me to carry.*
*I stood by Daddy on Christmas morn,*
*Who acted a little scared.*
*With tears forming in his eyes,*
*He muttered a little prayer.*
*Glory to God on high,*
*For what you have done for us.*
*From the bottom of our hearts, dear God,*
*Comes a very, merry Christmas.*

## Parent Talk

For the most part, mothers are easier to talk with than fathers. Case in point: Reverend Harley. He and his wife were separated—two children, boy age 8, and a girl 11-going-on 15. Mother helped two days a week, had lots of conferences with the teachers, and was on top of what was happening at school with the kids. Son spent weekend with Dad, who had been a no-show at school until now.

Son tells Dad that he is being picked on. (I don't know why he referred to himself as Reverend Harley because he told me that he worked for the Internal Revenue Service.) In any case, he showed up Monday morning, ready to take on everyone. He was about 6'5", weighed more than 300 pounds, and used his height, weight, and loud, booming voice to his advantage. He pretty much told me what was going to happen if I didn't put a stop to his son getting picked on. He didn't ask any questions, such as "Do you know anything about what's going on?" He made his one statement and walked out.

It was three days later, no school for kids, and I was in the media center in the middle of an inservice session with teachers. The secretary interrupted my inservice to tell me that Reverend Harley was here to talk to me. I told her to tell Reverend Harley that I was busy right now but would be free in about 15 minutes. She returned about five minutes later and told me that Reverend Harley said that if I was not downstairs within three minutes, that I would have to call the police because he would be breaking up everything in my office.

Common sense tells me now that I should've been scared, but instead, I was really angry with this arrogant man. I took the steps two at a time — I could do that then — stormed into my office and shouted, "Reverend Harley, don't you ever..." He held up his hand to stop me from talking, and then he started laughing. He said sit down. I sat. Then he thanked me for taking care of the situation with his son and said we now needed to talk about his daughter. Reverend Harley and I were good pals all of a sudden. He then told me what was obvious. He was black and his wife was white. He said that when a child was from a biracial family, that when the child reached a certain age, he or she could choose which race he or she preferred to be identified with. He said that this issue was part of the tension between his wife and him. And then he talked some more about his daughter and of his concerns for her at this stage of her life. And then I saw a different Reverend Harley than the man I had met a few days ago. He was struggling to help his children with their identity, remorseful over the separation from his wife, and seeking help wherever he could find it. I could do nothing for this man but listen and assure him that we would do our best for them here at school.

## Children's Book Week

Children's Book Week was big at New Market. Carol Beall, our media specialist, would come up with something crazy for me to do if kids read for a specific number of hours. Over the years, I have spent a day on the roof of our school, sat in a boat on a pond next to our school for a day, walked a pig on a leash for a day, dressed and posed as a Power Ranger, had tractor races with an assistant, and led the student body in dancing the Macarena and the Chicken Dance.

This was over a period of years. I would wear signs that read, "I don't want to go up on that roof — watch TV tonight — don't read." And what we wanted to happen always did — the kids read and turned in their hours. I believed that if we could convince kids to read more, they would find out that recreational reading was far more enjoyable to them than watching TV for countless hours. The stunts I did were always fun, although I did reject Carol's suggestion one year that I go up in a hot air balloon.

A few days before I was scheduled to walk the pig on a leash, I received an anonymous note, telling me that this would be too much stress on the pig and I should cancel that activity. If I didn't, I would be reported to the group dealing with cruelty to animals. (I wasn't going to ride or kiss the pig; I was just going to walk him.) Cindy Bell, great teacher and pig farmer who provided the pig for the day, assured me that I would be doing no harm to her pig.

## Straight As and Os

In elementary school, grades one, two, and three receive O, S, and U on report cards. Grades four and five receive A, B, C, and D. The first year I came to New Market, only six students received either all Os or all As. As an incentive, I told the kids that everyone who got all Os or all As on their report card would get a personal letter of congratulations from me, inviting them to have lunch with me on a specific day, and after lunch, having an ice cream treat on me. Ten years later, I was having lunch and buying ice cream for 60 to 80 students every grading period.

## Hat Day

I had this thing about kids wearing hats inside the school building. I just didn't like it. I told my assistant that I was going to come up with something to stop it, short of demanding it. He told me that I wouldn't be able to get the kids to stop wearing hats willingly, and he also said that my head was stuck in the sand. He told me it was the '90s, and kids do things differently now.

Teachers were allowed to have casual dress day on Fridays. One morning, I said to the kids over the intercom: "You know that teachers don't have to dress up on Fridays. I think Friday ought to be a special day for kids too. From now on, you will be able to wear hats inside the school building on Fridays; Monday through Thursday, you may not. I hope that you think that this is fair." At lunch that day, I asked them to raise their hands if they could support my request to wear hats just one day a week. It was practically unanimous.

## Big Brother Is Watching

I was always visible before and after school and during every lunch period. Kids loved to come up and give me a hug, and I would hug them back. I had a boss once who told me that I should not allow kids to hug me, and I certainly should not hug them. He said that people would read wrong things into my hugs. I thought about that for about two days and then resumed hugging. I had been doing it for 25 years, knowing that I had only the right intentions, and I didn't plan to stop now.

The same boss called later to tell me of another habit I had, which he said should be stopped. For more than 15 years, whenever anyone received straight As or Os and I wrote them their congratulatory letters, I always ended the letters by writing, "Love, Mr. Shade." The boss told me that a board member had been called by a parent and asked if he was aware that a principal was using the word "love" in his letters to kids. The boss told me that, in this day and age, those letters could be harmful to me and misinterpreted by parents. I told him that I understood what he was saying, and I meant no disrespect to his suggestion, but if I had to stop doing two things I loved to do, then I would have to leave. I couldn't draw a line over which neither the kids nor I could cross. Maybe this was also a sign of the 90s. Be careful what you do and say; one misstep and you are up to your neck in litigation. One side of me really understood the importance of taking this matter seriously; another side of me resented that "somebody downtown" would tell me now, after 25 years of trying to become the best principal and person I could be to these kids, that I should change my style because people were watching.

## Childbirth 201
A few years ago, a very pregnant second-grade teacher came into my office. She pulled two chairs close together, sat in one, and propped her feet up on the other. She looked at me and said, "Tom, I'm about to have this baby, and you are going to have to help deliver it." I didn't know whether she was kidding or not, but I know I had her husband on the phone and then at my school within minutes.

## Emergency
That incident made me nervous, but this next one really scared me. We received a telephone call one evening stating that a high school bus had been involved in an accident, several kids had been taken to the hospital, and at least one was in serious condition. The caller also said that the one student believed to be the most serious was the son of one of my second-grade teachers. I told the teacher the news, and

as she grabbed her purse and car keys, I took the keys and told her that I was driving.

We talked about everything and nothing on the way in. About a block from the hospital, I noticed that she had her hand on the door handle. I said, "Marcy, I am going to pull into the parking space, and I want you to take your hand off the door handle until the car is stopped." She said okay, but her hand remained there. We did stop the car and raced to the emergency room. I could have left her out of the car by the emergency room door, but I didn't want her to go in by herself. Entering the area where the kids from the accident were, the first words we heard were, "Hi, Mom." It was her son, and he was okay.

## Observations

I don't think teachers always liked my sense of humor. After every formal observation, I would write it up and then have the teacher come in to discuss it. It would be signed by both of us, and a copy would go downtown to be placed in the teacher's permanent file. I only did this next thing when a teacher had a particularly good lesson. The teacher didn't know yet that I thought it was a good lesson. When she came into the office, I asked her to sit down and then I would reach around, pick up my box of Kleenex, and place it between the teacher and me. (I still hadn't said a word.) Then I would pick up the observation and pretend to be studying it before I gave it to the teacher to read. Most laughed at my attempt at humor; some didn't.

## The Dog Is In The Alley

Teachers pulled a few things too. Teachers knew that when I was walking around with a clipboard in my hands, that I was observing, but they didn't always know where I was going next. I always thought it strange that when I went into a room to observe, a child would immediately walk out with a note in his or her hand. It took me a long time before I found out that teachers had their own little secret message system for letting each other know when I was in their area doing observations. The message on the note always said, "Watch out, the dog is in the alley."

## A Misconstrued Phrase

It was our annual kindergarten orientation meeting, and there were probably 150 parents in the room, most of them sending children to school for the first time. Earlier that day, as one of the parents was registering her child, a teacher came in with an unruly student. The teacher sat him in a chair and told the secretary "to have Tom give him a good one when he comes in." I knew exactly what the teacher meant, although no one should be saying something that could be so easily misconstrued. The teacher and I had talked about this child the day before and I had told her that if he caused trouble the next day, send him to the office and I would give him "a good talking to." I did talk to the boy later, but I was not told exactly what the teacher said when she brought him to the office.

At the meeting that night, I was going over all the things these new parents needed to hear. Betty Jeffers, my secretary, was sitting near the rear. She was in charge of refreshments. All of a sudden, a lady stood up and said, "I'd rather hear about the principal who beats kids." I went into slight shock as the lady repeated the statement, only louder this time. I looked at Betty and my eyes were saying, "Do you know anything about this?" In a very quiet voice—by that time it didn't matter how quiet she was, you could hear a pin drop—she said, "I'll tell you later." I looked at her, then looked at all the parents looking at me, and said, "Betty, I think you had better tell me about it right now." Betty explained what had happened, and I explained what I had told the teacher earlier. I think they all went home satisfied with the explanations.

### Overcrowding
As I became older (and hopefully, wiser), I felt that it was important in a school, especially one that had 13 portable classrooms and more than 1,000 students (450 over capacity), to attempt to create a climate that would keep morale high. The teachers and staff at New Market became family. Many parents would tell us that they could sense the positive atmosphere of our school as soon as they walked in the front door. Teachers shared knowledge and communicated with each other. A very jovial Bobby Garver, often wearing her huge pig bedroom slippers, greeted the students every morning as soon as they got off the bus.

When students did something wrong, they knew that any adult in the building would stop them and correct them. Fair, firm, consistent, and immediate discipline was important. Consequences were appropriate to the infractions. Even though discipline does not always make people happy, it does let everybody know what will not be tolerated. When the principal can greet practically every kid by name, eat with them at lunchtime, and listen to them when they talk about their concerns, they feel good about him/her and themselves. When you had staff and students walk in and out of the main building in heavy rain and snow, while going to and from portables; when you ate lunch at 10:30 in the morning because you were on first lunch shift, or at 1:30 in the afternoon because you were on last lunch shift; when you got caught in the crowded hallways when classes were coming to and leaving from lunch; when you had two gang bathrooms and three or four individual bathrooms in the whole school for more than 1,000 students, no bathrooms or running water in the portables, then you had better have some other things going for you that would make coming to this school a positive experience.

To their credit, our teachers never went to their union and complained; they never said, "I can't handle this;" they never said, "Let me transfer and get out of here." What they did say was, "Let's work together and do what has to be done to make New Market Elementary School a great place for parents to send their children." Parents, too, were overwhelmingly supportive. Concerns were raised often about how to get relief for our overcrowded schools, but no one placed any blame on the school administrators or school staff, nor was any extra pressure exerted. I remember a meeting at Linganore High School, chaired by Dave Markoe, to discuss options for relieving overcrowding at New Market. One of the options was to find temporary places to house a number of our students until the new school was built to relieve us. I know he was serious about this option because he told me to find the places. When the parents were asked about this option, their unanimous vote was for all of us to stay together at New Market until the new school was built.

I was just so proud to be part of that community when they gave us that endorsement. Teachers enjoyed working at New Market and Green Valley, and parents loved having their children attend those schools. That's a great combination.

During this time at New Market, a group of parents became active politically. They attended any and all meetings related to continued development in the county, their primary concern being all the overcrowded schools in the county. Working from New Market, they called themselves The Committee on Overcrowding. They were led by two very smart, savvy, articulate, and determined (some said hardheaded) women, Elaine Grove and Val Hertges. They became the watchdogs of education, majoring in home building and projection estimating. Developers and their lawyers groaned when Val and Elaine showed up at Planning and Zoning meetings. They were called names—"Mommy

Mongers" is one I can print.

Their work in our school district led to the formation of similar groups in other schools, which led to a larger group called ABC for Education.

In my heart, I rooted for this group to be successful. They were very instrumental in keeping the pressure on for the governor and the people working at the Interagency for School Construction in Annapolis to approve and appropriate funding for the new Deer Crossing Elementary School which would relieve congestion in our area. But as a mid-level manager for the school system, I was fully aware of who signed my paycheck and to whom I owed my allegiance and loyalty. It was not as if there were state secrets to give away, but both the Board of Education and ABC for Education were working hard to help us, and I didn't want to do anything that would jeopardize either one's progress. The parents in the group were very aware of my position and never asked me to do anything that would create a conflict of interest.

## Year 'Round School

Because so many of our schools were overcrowded, it was essential that our system look at alternative ways of providing relief. To that end, I was asked by the superintendent of schools to serve on the Year 'Round School Advisory Committee to determine if this was a concept we could recommend for our board to pursue.

Year 'Round School did not mean that students would attend school all year long. It meant that the schedule would be configured so that the building would be used year 'round and that some percentage of students would always be attending school. Students would still need to attend school for 180 days, but not all at the same time.

The most popular of the year 'round schedules seemed to be the 45-15 plan. The schedule was drawn up for different groups and for different times of the year. Theoretically, parents could choose their schedule. No matter which schedule you chose, your child would go to school for 45 school days and then be on break for 15 days. It would start again until four cycles of 45 school days were completed. The traditional two-month summer break would be gone, which upset many parents. Proponents of a year 'round plan argued that parents could now choose a plan that gave them a winter break, if that's what they wanted. Those in doubt about the plan argued that children from the same families could be on different school schedules.

Our county could have been an example of that. The initial reasoning was that we were looking for ways to relieve crowding at the elementary schools. If a year 'round plan had been accepted, my guess would be that it would have affected elementary only; middle and high schools would have remained on their regular schedules, at least at first. There would have been some cost savings by using the buildings year 'round, but there would have been just as much expense, if not more, because more teachers and support staff would have to have been hired to provide full-time 12-month staffs. Cleaning and maintenance would have to have been done at night.

Our committee recommended against initiating a year 'round plan. We felt that it would create as many problems as it would solve. Also, a huge concern was that continuity of programs and academic achievement appeared to be weak at those schools where we observed year 'round models first-hand.

*Here's to the kids who are different*
*The kids who don't always get As*
*The kids who have ears*
*Twice the size of their peers*
*And noses that go on for days.*

*Here's to the kids who are different*
*The kids they call crazy and dumb*
*The kids who aren't cute*
*And don't give a hoot*
*Who dance to a different drum.*

*Here's to the kids who are different*
*The kids with the mischievous streak*
*For when they have grown*
*As history has shown*
*It's their difference that makes*
*them unique.*

Anonymous

# Inclusion

It was a Sunday night, and Dr. Michele Krantz called me at home to tell me that Dr. Carol Quirk of the Maryland Coalition for Inclusive Education (MCIE) would be at my school the next day to talk to me about inclusion. I had no idea what the word meant, but after Carol's talk, I was very interested. The basic premise was that students with disabilities who previously had attended special schools for the handicapped (in our county, Rock Creek), can now attend the school they would have gone to if they did not have a disability, and with access to extra curricular activities. There were eight children who lived in our school district and who attended Rock Creek at that time.

Before any of the children attended our school, MCIE staff trained us. Our lead trainer, Marcie Roth, was committed to inclusion, and a great motivator as well. There were many new skills to be learned:

- Collaboration — Regular classroom teachers of children with disabilities collaborate and plan with the special education teacher to design a program for a broad range of abilities.
- Accommodations — Once the program for instruction for the broad range of abilities is designed, teachers make accommodations for individual students.
- Adapt and Co-Teach — Curriculum must be adapted to meet everybody's needs. Teachers and other adults quite often co-teach the students in the class where special services are needed.

Once our training was completed, we were ready to go. No teacher was required to accept a student with disabilities. I asked for volunteers, and Janet Manning was the first. Dawn Irwin was the special education teacher. Brian had autism, and he was our first inclusion student; his aide was Anne Olsen. In our county, a student would be eligible for aide help if there were safety or health concerns. Janet planned for her class the same way she always had. Dawn would look at those plans and make the necessary accommodations for Brian, and Anne would implement those accommodations. It was a true collaborative effort. They became so good as a team that during their second year of inclusive practices, they were invited to teacher-training workshops in many other counties in Maryland.

If I live to be 100, I will never forget Valerie. Valerie has Down's syndrome. She is funny, smart, manipulative, and hardheaded. I remember two incidents concerning Val. She had a very special friend in third grade. We encouraged our non-inclusion students to join the Circle of Friends for our students with disabilities. They would help them with their work, eat lunch with them, and play with them outside. There is no doubt in my mind that our "regular" children profited much from their association with our children with disabilities. They learned about differences, about acceptance, and a lot about helping others. There was never one instance in our experiences where we had any cases of teasing or making fun of other kids.

Initially, we thought that some children might shy away from interacting and developing friendships with students with disabilities. Nothing could have been further from the truth. A fourth-grade girl wrote, "As a nine-year-old girl, I have learned to make friends with children who have special needs. Some of the things I like doing with my special friends is play when it is recess, or working in the classroom. I learn a lot from them. I learned how a Communication Book works from helping a girl with autism.

I like when my friends look at me and smile and I just like when my friends with autism come out of their little world.

I heard my friend with autism say to her aide, with no help at all, 'Haffy Birtday.' It made everyone break out and cry. They were so happy, even when I heard, I cried.

When I was little, I was scared of kids who were different. After I had the chance to get to know kids who were different, I began to accept them for who they are.

My friend with Down's syndrome was working on the computer by himself. I went over to him and asked if he needed any help.

Just like any other 10- or 11-year-old boy would do, he turned around and said, 'GET LOST!' I giggled."

Val's reading group was working at the front of the class with the teacher; the girl friend was working at her desk, which was located immediately behind where Val was sitting; I was in the classroom, walking around. Val stood while answering a question from the teacher, receiving praise for a correct answer. Without turning around, Val put her hands behind her back and proceeded to back up. When she got close to the desk behind her, the friend, without looking up, reached out and touched Val's hand. Val then moved forward and sat down. If this was the kind of thing that would happen under inclusion, I was all for it.

A few weeks later, I was in that classroom again, doing a formal observation of the teacher, Marcy Jubach. A few minutes into the lesson, Val had to go to the bathroom. Quite a few minutes later, Val had not returned, and the teacher was looking at her watch. A short time later, I heard her say, "Boys and girls, excuse me, please read the next chapter quietly; I'll be right back." The teacher looked at me, rolled her eyes, and then went to her desk and picked up what looked like an egg timer. I didn't realize until later that Valerie would sometimes go to the bathroom and sit humming to herself. Valerie's bathroom buddy was not in school that day, and probably because the teacher did not want to interrupt the observation, she allowed Val to go by herself.

Marcy walked out of the room with the egg timer. Out of curiosity, I followed her. The girls' bathroom was right next to the classroom. Standing in the hallway, I heard Marcy say, "Valerie, just because your friend is not here today is no reason not to take your timer with you. Now let me show you again. There, did you hear that bell ring? Good, because that means that you get off the seat and return to your classroom." On their way back, Val said, "Hi, Mr. Shade." Marcy didn't look at me. Sometimes, good lessons don't always come from a textbook. What I overheard between the teacher and student was as good a teaching-learning experience as any, and I marked her observation accordingly.

There were several reasons why inclusion was successful in our school. Probably, the main one was that, I, as the principal, totally supported the concept. (Research states that the principal is the main ingredient for failure or success.) Second, the teachers, after having been trained, did not feel threatened or intimidated. They learned that if everyone on the collaboration team did his/her job, then no one person's workload became too much.

Teachers were making the extra effort to make this work, and it was happening right at the time when we were our most heavily populated, more than 1,000 students. As is usually the case, the principal would reap the benefits of any success. I was invited to national conferences to speak on inclusion, to statewide workshops and seminars, to work with administrators and teachers just beginning, and the ultimate was the invitation to speak and participate in a meeting designed to solicit input and feedback from the disability and education communities. The meeting was held in the Senate Russell Caucus room at the Russell Senate Building in Washington, D.C. David Hobby, chief of staff for Senate Majority Leader Trent Lott, conducted the meeting. The purpose of the meeting was for people to speak for or against the continued funding of the Individuals with Disabilities Education Act (IDEA). IDEA is a civil rights statute that conveys upon children with disabilities and their parents a number of legal rights. I was so nervous while waiting to speak. I shared with the committee the many successful experiences our school had while working with children with disabilities and spoke to the continued funding of IDEA. The nervousness changed to smiles after I had given my talk when Senator Lott's chief of staff, and others in attendance, interested in schools with students with disabilities, asked if they could visit our school. I couldn't wait until I got back to share this wonderful news with my staff.

The visit was set up for approximately a month from that day. The visiting group would include representatives of several congressmen and senators, as well as people representing inclusion and special education at the Maryland State Department of Education. My staff was excited and looking forward to the visit. But several people at our central office didn't appear to be as excited. During the next few weeks, I received telephone calls from our legal department and from supervisors in our special education department. I was asked, "Tom, what did you say to those people in Washington? You do realize, don't you, that you do not speak for, nor do you represent Frederick County's policy on special education issues? Send to us immediately, a list of names and titles of those people who will be visiting your school. Also, send us a written statement outlining exactly what you plan to say to these people when they come."

I knew immediately that this was another one of those times when my superiors were uneasy about what I was saying to outsiders about our school program, and they were not confident in my ability to speak about our successes, without it reflecting poorly for our system in some way. This was another instance where I became involved in the "politics of education." Their defensive attitude confused me. If they had bothered to read the comments I had made to this committee or to any of the other groups to whom I had been asked to speak, they would have known immediately that I never said anything about inclusion except what was happening in *my own school*. I would never pretend to be a spokesperson for inclusion or special education in our county.

In my mind, I did what I was initially asked to do, and that was to learn about inclusion and then help my staff develop and implement a successful program in our school for children with disabilities. I never went beyond my authority and my immediate bosses always knew what we were doing. If they felt that I was "getting in over my head," then the successful program at New Market caused that to happen. We disagreed on some things, but I had always taken pride in the fact that I considered myself to be an extremely loyal employee of the superintendent and the school system. Parents, students, and staff contributed to a program that was being recognized and complimented by educators well outside our system.

Our system was proud of us too, until we got to a level that they perceived to be beyond our competence. It ended well, I thought. On the day of the visit, there were some high-level visitors from downtown, staying in the background, and listening carefully to what I, and others, had to say. I summarized my previous talk about successful inclusive practices at New Market Elementary School, and then introduced students with and without disabilities to the audience, and had them explain and demonstrate why inclusion worked so well at our school. My superiors congratulated me after the presentation. I hope that I convinced them that day that all I had ever been interested in was creating good learning opportunities and successful experiences for all of our children, regardless of their race, gender, or disability.

Right about this same time, I was asked by TASH, a national disability advocacy group, to be one of the presenters at a national inclusion conference in San Francisco. TASH would pay my expenses. My talk was on inclusion but would center specifically on a student named Sam, who had autism, and the methods we used to make his transition from Rock Creek to New Market Elementary to New Market Middle so successful. My co-presenters were Marcie Roth and Steve Parsons from New Market Middle School.

In preparation for my talk, I had asked my fifth-grade team to make a tape for me so that I could let my audience hear some live voices explaining their strategies for Sam. In fact, I would begin my talk by playing excerpts of one of their discussions. They didn't make one tape; they made two. Their first tape had everything I needed when they played it for me at home. But what they gave me for my presentation, unbeknownst to me, was the second tape. When I turned on the tape player, the voice said to the audience, "Hello, ladies and gentlemen, we are Tom's teachers back in New Market, Maryland, still working very hard so that Tom can go to San Francisco and other places and describe our great inclusion program. Have a good time, Tom. If you need us, we'll be here—all day, every day." The audience roared acceptance at this unplanned greeting.

My only regret about inclusion is that we didn't start it earlier in my career. Carmen and Maria registered their daughter, Lauren, at our school. Lauren was legally blind and paralyzed on one side of her body. When I was taking her and her parents around our school, Lauren accidentally stepped on my foot. She glanced toward me and said, "Excuse me, I wasn't watching where I was going." I had known her for 10 minutes and already liked her a lot.

Lauren joined our fifth-grade chorus, which had been invited to sing at the annual Dr. Martin Luther King program. Julie Weaver Seiler, our music teacher, had told Joyce Harris, moderator of the program, that this would be my last one before retiring. When our chorus was introduced, Joyce told the audience that my students had requested that I come on stage and be with them during their performance. Lauren was at the end of the front row, and I walked over to stand by her. When I got there, she handed me a red rose and kissed me on the cheek; then both of us sang with the chorus, both off-key, holding hands and crying.

I feel I was blessed to have had the opportunity to work with, and learn about, these truly amazing children with multiple handicaps and disabilities. Parents felt that their children who were attending a regular public school for the first time, were coming home happy, were not being teased at school nor in the neighborhood, were being invited to birthday parties for the first time, were being overwhelmingly accepted by all children and adults, and were learning skills in school commensurate with their ability. Many parents shared with me that these wonderful experiences gave them increased hope, not despair, for the future of their children.

## Children Learn What They Live

If a child lives with criticism,
He learns to condemn.
If a child lives with hostility,
He learns to fight.
If a child lives with ridicule,
He learns to be shy.
If a child lives with shame,
He learns to feel guilty.
If a child lives with tolerance,
He learns to be patient.
If a child lives with encouragement,
He learns confidence.
If a child lives with praise,
He learns to appreciate.
If a child lives with fairness,
He learns justice.
If a child lives with security,
He learns to have faith.
If a child lives with approval,
He learns to like himself.
If a child lives with acceptance and friendship,
He learns to find love in the world.

Anonymous

# Recognition

I have received many awards and honors during my career.

While at Green Valley Elementary School, I was given the Lifetime Achievement Award by the National Congress of PTAs. I have been told that I was the first recipient from Frederick County to receive this honor. This was in 1978.

In 1989, I received the TV Channel 13 Salute of Maryland's Most Beautiful People. Parents and students of New Market Elementary School nominated me.

In 1994, the Frederick County Association of Educational Secretaries and Assistants bestowed on me their Administrator of the Year Award.

In 1995, I received the *Washington Post* Distinguished Educational Leadership Award. I was presented with a Waterford Crystal school bell and a trip to the Virgin Islands for my wife and me. Mary Spanberger, president of the Maryland Congress of PTAs, nominated me.

In 1996, I was asked by my PTA president to go to Baltimore to be present for a surprise award being given to Bobby Garver by the Maryland PTA group. When the awards were announced, my name was read as the person to receive the State PTA Educator of the Year Award. Bobby received her award and she was as surprised as I was because she thought she was there only to witness my award.

In the spring of 1997, some former elementary students at New Market visited me after school one day. These young ladies and gentlemen were currently seniors at Linganore High School. They started reminiscing about some experiences we had together. Then one of them said that the group was going to recommend to Mr. Trout that I should be invited to the high school for some of their senior activities. I told them that just their coming back to visit me was enough to make me happy.

About a month later, Mike Trout, principal at Linganore High, called me and told me that the 1997 Linganore High School class would like me to come to their graduation ceremony to be honored and recognized as their elementary school principal. To be asked by these young men and women to attend their graduation ceremony seven years after they left my school was indeed an honor. To be sitting on the stage watching their smiling faces on the most wonderful evening of their young lives was without a doubt one of the proudest moments of my career. I felt so good to share their happiness.

In late spring of 1997, I was asked to speak for the continued funding of the Individuals with Disabilities Education Act (IDEA), at the Russell Senate Office building in Washington, D.C. David Hobby, chief of staff for Senate Majority Leader Trent Lott, conducted the meeting.

As anyone would be, I was flattered, honored, pleased, and grateful for all of the recognition. When things go well at a school, the principal usually gets the accolades. None of these awards would have happened without the overwhelming support of parents and teachers, and I owe them a great debt of gratitude. And lastly, to the thousands of kids who have touched my life over these years, and without whom these honors wouldn't exist, thank you and I love you.

*To A Special Teacher*

*If you're convinced*
*that lessons are appealing*
*And you do your best*
*to help each student learn,*
*If you can give and give*
*and keep on feeling*
*That their success*
*rewards you in return,*
*If you believe there is*
*no greater pleasure*
*Than doing just exactly*
*what you do,*
*Then you're a student's*
*greatest lifelong treasure—*
*A teacher who is special*
*through and through*

Anonymous

# Afterword

I have been praised and recognized, threatened, and scolded over the last 30 years, but nothing could have given me more pleasure than I got from working with teachers and children. I certainly made the right career choice.

I will end with a quote from an unknown author. The message could well be written about any one of the hundreds of teachers and educators that I have had the privilege of working with.

"A HUNDRED YEARS FROM NOW, IT WILL NOT MATTER WHAT MY BANK ACCOUNT WAS, THE SORT OF HOUSE I LIVED IN, OR THE KIND OF CAR I DROVE ... BUT THE WORLD MAY BE DIFFERENT BECAUSE I WAS IMPORTANT IN THE LIFE OF A CHILD."

*Thomas H. Shade*
*March 2000*